"How can I meet and marry a country music star?"

No matter how much money and prestige accompany being married to a celebrity, there is the element of regularly feeling like a single married woman. Most wives in the following pages know what it's like not to know the whereabouts of their traveling husbands at 2:00 A.M. They know firsthand the frustration of having to handle crises with children while their husbands are on the road. They've had to live with damaging reports about their husbands' behaviors that are often no more than published lies. They know what it's like to wait for a month for a man to come home for two days.

And then he spends them sleeping.

—from the Foreword by Tom Carter

"Will satisfy the curiosity of avid fans."

—*Library Journal*

"Pour a mug of coffee, pop in your favorite country CD and read the reflections and comments by these women who, while having lives of luxury beyond their wildest dreams, you probably wouldn't want to trade places with."

—*Providence Sunday Journal*

Nashville WIVES

**COUNTRY MUSIC'S CELEBRITY WIVES
REVEAL THE TRUTH ABOUT
THEIR HUSBANDS AND MARRIAGES**

Mrs. George Jones

AND TOM CARTER

HarperPaperbacks
A Division of HarperCollinsPublishers

HarperPaperbacks
A Division of HarperCollins*Publishers*
10 East 53rd Street, New York, NY 10022-5299

ISBN 0-06-103006-6

HarperCollins®, 📖®, and HarperPaperbacks™
are trademarks of HarperCollins Publishers, Inc.

Cover photographs:
Billy Ray and Tish Cyrus is a Cyrus family photo.
Used by permission. Garth and Sandy Brooks is a photo by
Judy Mock. Used by permission. Glen and Kim Campbell
is a Campbell family photo. Used by permission.

A hardcover edition of this book was published in 1998 by
Cliff Street Books, an imprint of HarperCollins*Publishers.*

First HarperPaperbacks printing: December 1999

Printed in the United States of America

Visit HarperPaperbacks on the World Wide Web at
http://www.harpercollins.com

❖ 10 9 8 7 6 5 4 3 2 1

Contents

Acknowledgments

I'm indebted to my husband, George Jones, for putting up with all the time I took away from managing his career to work on my own. He's as understanding as he is talented.

I obviously appreciate the cooperation of some very busy wives. One can't write a book about Nashville wives without the involvement of those wives. Amid the pressures of maintaining a marriage and rearing children, the wives met with me or my coauthor, Tom Carter, on many occasions. Thank you, ladies.

Special thanks to Debbie Doebler, my business manager and friend. An old rule says one person can't be both. Debbie proves that rule is wrong. I love her like a sister.

Thanks to Evelyn Shriver, who has been George's and my publicist for more years than either of us cares to remember. Her resignation from publicity came on the very day the first draft of this book was finished. I wonder if the one had anything to do with the other. She became president of Asylum Records, so that company now has the female gender's answer to Donald Trump as its leader.

Thanks to Adina Estes, my daughter, for making copies of the hundreds of photographs that were considered for this project. I'm grateful to Jane Hailey for helping to secure original pictures from wives scattered around the nation.

Tom Carter and I have worked together on two books and are considering a third. He is my associate and friend.

—Mrs. George Jones

ACKNOWLEDGMENTS

I appreciate the hospitality of Stella Howard and her staff at the Hampton Inn in Murfreesboro, Tennessee, where I stayed for the five days of privacy needed to finish the manuscript. Special thanks to Linda Cramer for making the arrangements.

I appreciate the moral support from Rebecca Holden and Travis Carter, and the research and legwork by Jane Hailey. Bill Robinson has a sharp eye when searching for typographical errors.

Dean Williamson was an ideal agent in that he never complained about my complaining. This is our second book. He may soon leave publishing to go into psychology after so much practical experience with a neurotic.

Diane Reverand is the perfect editor. She stays far enough away from a project to see its faults, yet close enough to correct them. I'd write for her anytime.

I'm grateful to Evelyn Shriver, who negotiated the terms of the Rhonda Adkins chapter. It would have never been written without Evelyn, who should moonlight as a diplomat.

I appreciate the wives, most of whom had the courage to be honest and the wisdom to be tactful.

Finally, a heartfelt thank-you to Nancy Jones for staying with this undertaking when a lot of temperamental wives could have tempted her to leave it. Nancy and I worked together on her husband's autobiography, *I Lived to Tell It All*, by George Jones. She saved his career, and she's beginning to do wonders for mine.

—Tom Carter

Foreword

I have cowritten nine books in nine years that were largely the result of reader request. I live in Nashville, Tennessee, where I am regularly exposed to country music fans, many of whom don't hesitate to ask personal questions about their favorite singers. It's easy to determine about whom they'd like to read.

I eventually realized that the questions I was hearing frequently pertained not to the male superstars, but to their wives.

"What is Garth Brooks's wife really like?" was a recurring probe. "Do you know Mrs. Alan Jackson? How did she meet Alan?" "Does Mrs. Billy Ray Cyrus cook and clean house?" "Does Mrs. John Michael Montgomery think that he cheats, since he's so handsome and all?" "Does Mrs. Kenny Rogers worry about the age difference with her husband?"

You get the idea.

Perhaps the question I've heard most frequently has come from single women.

"How can I meet and marry a country music star?" many have wanted to know.

I've traveled the United States and Canada with many country luminaries, and whenever I'm on the road, the questions about the Nashville wives continue. I don't think I've ever had an extended conversation about a male star without eventually being asked about his wife, if he had one.

The idea of writing a book about Nashville's celebrity wives was an idea whose time had come, and was even overdue.

I didn't want to simply interview the wives. That seemed clinical and impersonal. I wanted to get to know those I did not already know personally. I had dined in many of their homes, had traveled in their tour buses, and had even held their youngsters. Nonetheless, I figured many wives would not talk to me as openly as they would talk to one of their peers, another Nashville wife.

So I approached the dean of Nashville wives, Mrs. George (Nancy) Jones, and asked if she'd like to write a book about the wives and let me assist. She thought long and hard. She was familiar with my work, as I had written a book with George in 1995. The text had been frank, and she wondered how eager the wives would be to talk frankly about their marriages. Would they regard this project as intrusive? Would she make enemies of her friends? How candid should the text be?

Nancy and I talked intermittently for about a year, then embarked on the project in the winter of 1997. We soon discovered an interesting quandary. Some of the wives would talk only to Nancy. They were shy in front of me, even though their remarks were eventually going to be made public. Nancy interviewed those women by herself. Others wanted to be interviewed only by me for the same reason in reverse. They were embarrassed about discussing personal things in front of Nancy, their friend. They found intimate talk easier with a comparative stranger. I often asked those wives questions from a list that Nancy helped prepare. Nancy similarly often asked wives questions from a list prepared by me. Two wives wanted to meet me without Nancy in a hotel room. That setting is not unusual for personal talk due to the obvious privacy. Still others wanted to be inter-viewed simultaneously by both Nancy and me, and they were.

The word *interview* is a misnomer. We often simply visited with some of the wives over lunch or hung out in their homes. Some wives wanted to chat in the presence of their husbands, but most did not. Others were uneasy about discussing their marriages face-to-face with either Nancy or me, and wanted to talk on the telephone. Nancy and I did separate telephone interviews and conference calls.

All conversations were tape-recorded.

The result, I think, is an astonishingly candid book. I've been surprised at what some of these wives have been willing to tell about themselves and their husbands.

If I have one regret, it's that too much time is spent talking about the husbands and not enough about the wives. "If it weren't for our husbands, you wouldn't want to talk to us," noted Barbara Brooks, wife of Kix Brooks of Brooks & Dunn. She has a valid point.

Many wives, after being asked to talk about their lives, talked only about their husbands because their husbands *are* their lives. They freely said so.

In some ways, this project was the most difficult I've ever undertaken. Many women, on one hand, wanted to be honest. On the other, they wanted to maintain appear-ances.

A popular misconception about Nashville wives is that they live on easy street. Not true. No matter how much money and prestige accompany marriage to a celebrity, there is the element of regularly being a single married woman. Most wives in the following pages know what it's like not to know the whereabouts of their traveling husbands at 2:00 A.M. They know first-hand the frustration of having to handle crises with children while their husband is on the road. They've had to live with damaging reports about a husband's behavior that are often no more than published lies. They know what it's like to wait for a month for a man to come home for two days.

And then he spends them sleeping.

I made some genuine friendships with some of the wives despite the fact that people often don't like portraits of themselves.

Some of the wives exhibited behavior that was difficult, if not impossible, before the writing process even began.

Nancy arranged an interview with one wife, for example, through her publicist. The publicist insisted that the wife would claim she had posed for a magazine that published nude photographs.

Sure enough, the woman said she posed, but said she decided against publishing the pictures, as she did not want to upset her father. Nancy and I wrote a chapter that included that information. The wife subsequently claimed she never said she posed.

I played her tape-recorded interview, and there were her own words saying she had posed. What was going on?

On the same tape, she said she had no inhibitions about nudity. The wife's actions and reactions were laced with so much apparent denial and so many apparent conflicts that Nancy and I elected not to put her in this book. I hate that. She was a pleasant, bright, and attractive woman whose candor, if it could have been sorted, would have been fascinating.

There was another wife who was among the most gracious women of all—at first. Nancy and I met her in her office. She wanted to see me again, and I returned without Nancy.

The wife was refreshingly open, and struggled to make her comments as clear and as accurate as possible. Nancy and I truly appreciated her intensity. We spent perhaps fifty hours writing and rewriting her chapter, and she continued to spoon-feed us information. She, through an assistant, called a half-dozen times.

Consequently, I felt I owed her something when someone attacked her marriage. The attacker wanted to know how to publish hurtful accusations. I would have no part of it.

The accuser claimed to be a representative of someone in the medical community who had allegedly treated the wife after repeated batterings by her husband.

I didn't believe that.

I tried to call the wife to warn her that the rumor was circulating. The accuser had credibility and wanted to sell the story to a national tabloid.

I talked to the wife's personal assistant, to a family member, and to someone on her management team. None would put me through to her. Some of the Nashville wives have inflated opinions of their importance. They see themselves as hillbilly Princess Dianas. I was earnestly trying to help a woman who had been good to me, and to thwart the battering junk before it found its way into print. But the wife was not about to take my call. She had simply become furious, not at the message, but at the messenger—me.

She called Nancy and said that I was "investigating" her. Investigating? I wasn't calling for purposes of publication. I was calling to *avoid* publication of false and damaging information. The wife apparently didn't understand, much less appreciate, the favor I was trying to do.

Enough about this book, and on to the book itself.

Besides, this isn't my book, anyhow. It is Nancy's, who participated in the writing and was made privy to every chapter and photograph before publication.

I, however, am solely responsible for this foreword.

—Tom Carter

Nashville WIVES

1

I met Mrs. Trace (Rhonda) Adkins through George's former publicist, the legendary Evelyn Shriver, a pillar of Nashville's publicity community, a one-woman answer to Hill and Knowlton. Evelyn handles the publicity for both George and Trace, among scores of other stars. Trace was a guest on George's weekly television show on the Nashville Network in February 1998. Rhonda and I chatted during the videotaping. I asked her to be a part of the Nashville Wives project because her story, like most of the wives', is incredible. She was one of the most open and outspoken of all of the wives. I was impressed by her honesty, particularly since she is a professional publicist who knew she was speaking on the record. During the interview, the tape recorder malfunctioned. She pointed that out, waited for repairs, then repeated some of the incredible things she had said earlier. She wanted to be sure they got on tape, delicate or not. She is one of the youngest of the Nashville wives. Perhaps her generation is more honest than older generations.

This darling lady has a personality that sparkles. She overflows with enthusiasm and joy. Most people in the Nashville music community, including me, are very fond of her.

* * *

The former Rhonda Forlaw was just trying to help. She pitched the talent of singer Trace Adkins to a record company president, and pointed out that the company's investment in Trace would be safe because he was a family man in stable surroundings.

But Trace missed his first appointment with the record company because his wife shot him. Rhonda immediately wondered about the stability of Trace's home life.

Here's how she tells the story of how she married one of country music's fastest-rising stars, the man with whom she intends to live forever.

She worked in publicity at Arista Nashville, the Clive Davis label brilliantly run by former University of Tulsa instructor Tim DuBois. Rhonda didn't work in the artists and repertoire division. She had nothing to do with signing new talent to the label. She was a publicist. It was not her official duty to look for new talent. She was just trying to help Trace, whom she didn't know, as well as her employer by matching the two. Her only motivation was the goodness of her heart.

She first heard Trace at a private party, and later went to hear him at a beer joint where he worked in Wilson County near Nashville. She was positive the guy had talent.

She had previously pitched an artist to the powers that be at Arista. They hadn't taken that artist seriously. He went on to record number-one records and garner major awards.

She wondered if she should pitch this Trace guy. Would she tap her boss's appreciation, or annoyance?

She decided to tell Tim about Trace. To her astonishment, Tim agreed to hear Trace in person. She took Tim to the beer joint, an establishment not found in a directory of five-star facilities.

"I can't believe I'm bringing my boss out to this place," she said, uneasy as Tim listened to Trace.

The record executive ended the evening by telling Rhonda she had good ears. He told her to tell Trace he wanted to meet him for lunch. She told Tim he wouldn't be sorry.

"I worried, Lord, have I wasted my boss's time or am I getting brownie points? I was so excited," she said. "So I went running back in, and I can be a bit overemotional at times, and I was all excited and his [Trace's] wife was right there with him. 'I can't believe this, you're going to have lunch with Tim DuBois next week!' And his wife and Trace were just standing there at the time and she was closed-armed and was staring at me, staring at me, just disgusted."

Tim DuBois had discovered Brooks & Dunn and Alan Jackson, among others. Rhonda felt that neither Trace nor his wife had any idea about the significance of dining with one of Nashville's true power brokers.

Rhonda left Trace and his wife with the understanding that Trace would call her the following Monday to schedule lunch with Tim. Trace didn't call. He was busy breathing, gasping for life while clinging to it in an intensive care unit.

It seems that Trace's wife shot him—through one lung, through the heart, and through the other lung.

The bullet broke through his ribs and fell onto the floor.

His first thought, said Rhonda, was that he was bleeding all over a new carpet. So he walked to a tile floor and collapsed so as not to stain the rug.

Rhonda's suspicions had been right. Trace was practical.

"So we were in this meeting [at Arista] and I get called out of the meeting for an urgent phone call and I take the phone call and the person tells me that the wife has shot Trace, and I had pitched the whole thing to Tim, 'stable artist, two children, wanted a recording deal his whole life.'"

"Why did his wife shoot him?" I asked.

"I don't know."

"You've never asked him?" Tom pressed.

"He doesn't know."

"Do you think she might have been jealous over the promise of the record deal?" I asked.

"Definitely," Rhonda said, "not a doubt in my mind."

"Do you think she was jealous of you?" I said.

"No, not jealous of me at all," Rhonda said. "I had only seen the man twice."

"But she was threatened by the fact that he was getting closer to a record deal and she didn't want him to be in the recording industry?" Tom probed.

"My perception," Rhonda answered. "But my first instinct when I found out he had been shot by his wife was, You jerk, what did you do to your little five-foot, one-inch wife, who weighed like one hundred pounds, to have her shoot you? I immediately took her side, I don't know why."

"You have pitched this guy as a model of mental stability and then you tell your boss that Trace can't have lunch with him because he's recovering from a gunshot wound?" Rhonda was asked.

"I immediately called my buddy who was a private detective," Rhonda explained. "I said, 'My reputation is on the line here.' "

She explained to the detective that she had thought she was a good judge of character, but perhaps had mistakenly endorsed a maniac. "So can you please find out whatever you can and let me know?" she asked the detective. "I want the facts, the truth.

"So he got into the files and read everything that happened, the police reports and everything, and called me back and said, 'Your buddy's not guilty. It's everybody's assumption that she just shot him and it was nuts.' "

When asked to deliver police reports and affidavits in connection with the incident for publication in this book, Rhonda referred the request to her manager, since she was busy having a baby. The manager declined to deliver the reports, and Evelyn called to say they would not be forthcoming.

The reports are public record.

More than three years after the shooting, and a short time after Rhonda married Trace, he was interviewed about the incident by reporters for *People* magazine.

Trace, then thirty-five, told a different story, one

that incriminated himself. The following was taken from the June 23, 1997, issue of *People*.

> As Adkins tells it, one February night in 1994 he and Julie Curtis, an insurance salesperson and [his] wife of three years, got into a shoving match when she accused him of breaking his promise to quit drinking beer. She tried to call her mother, he slapped the phone off the wall, and she grabbed the family's .38 from the top of the fridge.
>
> "Being a macho guy like I am, I tried to scare it out of her hand. I said, 'Give me the gun, or I'm gonna take it away from you and beat your damn brains out with it.' I would never have done that, but I told her in hopes that it would scare her.
>
> "The bullet . . . went through both my lungs and both ventricles of my heart," says Adkins, whose torso is laced with scars.

Several surgeries and a divorce followed. Adkins refused to press criminal charges. Rhonda said he was told that his insurance company would not pay his medical treatment if foul play were disclosed. She said Trace believed that.

Rhonda went to see Trace in the hospital where he was listed in critical condition for a month.

"I brought him flowers with Tim's blessing," Rhonda said, "because I figured if this was a person who had wanted to be a singer for ten years and his wife had just shot him, everything is going bad for this person.

"So I brought him this little basket of violets," she continued. "Purple has always been my favorite color and somehow I just remember this so vividly. I brought him a little basket of flowers and she [the wife] was in the room with him and his mother and I think his aunt, and I brought the flowers and he couldn't talk or anything."

Rhonda said that after Trace's hospital release, he wondered about the wisdom of not having pressed charges. She said she and Trace discussed it, and that she relayed the discussion to Tim. Rhonda feared that the record executive would be reluctant to invest a substantial amount of development money into a new artist who was about to enter a lawsuit.

"Trace, you need to go on with your life but I don't think that we can work with you," Rhonda told Trace.

She said Trace returned within two weeks to say that he was going to focus on his future, forgo criminal charges, and let the Lord handle the rest.

"Then what happened?" I wanted to know. That seemed to be the obvious and only question in this modern melodrama.

Rhonda said she spoke to Trace about three times during the next three months. In May, she invited him to a giant outdoor concert starring Brooks & Dunn. She thought it would inspire Trace to be around artists who had become successful on the record label that intended to sign him.

"Trying to give him something positive," she said. "He came out to that concert and he didn't even look like the same person. I mean, he had lost fifty or sixty pounds and had sunken cheeks. I didn't want anyone to see him because he didn't look like a potential star. He looked awful and was even having a hard time breathing."

She subsequently began to talk to Trace regularly about his delayed healing. It turned out that a hole in his heart wasn't mending.

"I was feeling sorry for this guy," she said. "So we decided that we would meet for dinner and I discovered that he was a great guy and we got along real well. And all of a sudden we start talking every day, just buddies, you know?"

Fan Fair, held annually in Nashville, is a week-long event with virtually nonstop activities for country music fans. Rhonda took Trace in June 1994. The festivity marked their first kiss.

There was no chance she would break his heart. It was already broken. Doctors announced that he would have to undergo a second round of open-heart surgery. The operation was successful, and Trace's recovery was accelerated.

"And now we're dating," Rhonda said. "And I didn't want Tim to know because now I'm dating this singer that I told him about. So Trace goes into the studio [to record for Arista]."

Trace did a showcase, and was at last signed to a development deal by Arista. Trace turned in the songs he'd recorded; Tim didn't like them, and told Rhonda. He suggested that she figure something out.

With guilt bearing down on her, she felt compelled to tell Tim, her employer of five years, that she had begun dating Trace. She apparently wanted Tim to think that romance was not affecting her objectivity about Trace's talents. She broke the news, and Tim said he had known it all along. Rhonda said Tim told her he could see it in her eyes.

Rhonda went out of town to a celebrity golf tournament. When she returned Trace picked her up at the airport. They ran into Scott Hendricks at the baggage claim area. Scott, who had formerly produced Brooks & Dunn, had become president of Capitol Nashville, the record label for Garth Brooks. Scott was impressed by Trace's speaking voice, and said he would be interested in signing him to a recording contract if he sang nearly as well as he spoke.

Once again, Rhonda took another record executive to the same dive where Tim had heard Trace. The first record executive had given Trace the development deal. Scott gave him a real recording contract on the spot, on the stage.

Trace Adkins, thanks to Rhonda's persistence, became the first Capitol Nashville signee under the Scott Hendricks administration.

Trace subsequently recorded "This Ain't No Thinkin' Thing" and "I Left Something Turned On," both of which became number-one songs. He recorded what became a top-five song, and won the Academy of Country Music's Top New Male Vocalist Award for 1997.

Rhonda began to tour with Trace on his one-night engagements, and soon they began living together.

"It was like we were husband and wife already,"

she said. "We were friends for that first six months but then after—the minute he kissed me—from then on I knew immediately this is the man I'm going to marry. I just knew. It was one of those weird deals. I really enjoy working with him. We're a team. I gave up my career at Arista Records to help him build a long-term career and a happy life together."

"Does he pay you?" I asked.

"He doesn't have to," she said. "We share everything and consider ourselves a team."

"But you're not on salary?" Tom queried.

"No," she said, "and I don't need to be. I trust him."

Sounds logical to me. George Jones doesn't pay me a salary either, and I've been his manager for years.

Now about the Trace/Rhonda marriage: This chapter makes me want to catch my breath, and I'm merely the author. These kids had as much trauma *before* their marriage as George and I had *during* ours.

Rhonda stood in the wings on November 23, 1996, when Trace debuted on the *Grand Ole Opry*, the world's longest-running live radio show. It is also televised. He had been incredibly nervous, even more than one might suspect of someone doing a premiere at the most historic of all country music entities. To make matters worse, through an astonishing breakdown in communications, no one remembered to tell Trace's band about the show. They didn't show up at what was the most important engagement of his career.

"Don't even plug in my guitar tonight," Rhonda related that Trace told the stage manager. "I'm too nervous to play."

"What do you mean?" she said the manager replied. "You're doing an acoustic set. Your band isn't coming."

Trace flipped and Rhonda paced.

Trace's first publicist had a copy of his only album in his car, parked three blocks away. She ran to the car, retrieved the album, and gave the song to "Bear," an old friend of Trace's who played in the Opry house band. Those musicians heard half of the song, walked on stage, and played an improvised version during Trace's debut at the Mother Church of country music.

Rhonda noticed that Trace wasn't wearing his jacket. Did he intend to go on stage without it? She stopped him and offered to retrieve it from his dressing room. The chaos was mounting, and reminded her of a Marx Brothers movie.

Trace barked for her to leave his jacket alone. She didn't know what to think. She didn't know he had entrusted the coat, and its contents, to someone else.

He finished his song, and embarked on a two-hour wait for the second show. He angrily called a meeting in his dressing room, and threw out everyone who wasn't a part of his management. He wanted to know where his band was. His two daughters had come to see their father debut. Rhonda took them ice skating at Opryland, an amusement park, until Trace's next performance.

By then, Trace's band had been notified, and had

arrived to play the show. Things were at last calm, Rhonda mistakenly thought.

The second show's audience received Trace with thunderous applause, and then the massive hall fell silent.

"I'd like to call my best friend out on the stage with me," Trace told the crowd.

"How sweet," Rhonda said, thinking Trace was referring to Bear, who'd played in his first band, and who now was on hand for the big debut.

Singer Marty Stuart suddenly began pulling Rhonda to the front of the stage. He shoved her from the safety of the darkened wings, directly into the spotlight of a nationally televised show.

She resisted, the crowd stirred, and everybody wondered what was going to happen next.

"You don't want me, you want Bear," Rhonda whispered to Marty. He just kept shoving her onto the stage.

Rhonda blinked in the spotlight in front of 4,400 people and a million television viewers. When her eyes cleared, she thought they were deceiving her.

Trace Adkins, at six feet, six inches tall, had dropped to his knees at center stage. In one hand he held his hat. In the other, he held a ring.

He asked her to marry him. She was stunned. She could see his lips moving, but she couldn't hear a thing.

Silence, followed by coughing and restlessness in the audience. So he asked again.

"For once in my life I was speechless," Rhonda recalled.

At last she said yes.

Trace saw her physically wilt as the applause rose. He picked her up and physically carried her off-stage before a standing ovation.

Dazed, Rhonda stepped into the wings. She babbled that she wished her parents could have seen this. Suddenly, her mother and father stepped out from nowhere. She smiled, then fainted dead away.

She later awakened, cradled in Trace's arms inside a hall swarming with security guards, relatives, performers, well-wishers, and others trying to revive her. Rhonda thought she was in a dream. She later decided it was a fairy tale.

They were married the following May in an outdoor wedding with eight hundred guests at the Belle Meade Plantation, a historic museum on whose lawn a Civil War battle was fought. Bullet holes dot the front door.

"I wanted to be Cinderella, and he didn't want a wedding at all," Rhonda said. "He just wanted to see a justice of the peace."

Rhonda's father picked out her wedding dress.

Trace sang at the reception. Having been a saloon singer, he was accustomed to taking requests. He facetiously sang a Merle Haggard classic entitled "Someday When Things Are Good, I'm Going to Leave You."

Her parents were not laughing as much as Trace was.

He had sung another song during the ceremony, which Rhonda had commissioned him to write. (He used cowriter Kenny Beard.) It was called "The Rest of Mine." In the song, the singer says he can't promise that he'll love his wife for the rest of her life, but he'll love her "for the rest of mine."

The song was subsequently released as a recording, and became number two in the nation.

Rhonda was reared in a prosperous household and attended good schools. She's from a pricey Chicago neighborhood, not a blue-collar southern community. She is an only child, born thirteen years into her parents' marriage. Yet disruption was her prenatal usher into this world.

Her mother lost thirteen pounds during a rocky pregnancy, Rhonda said.

"Every time she'd stand up she would hemorrhage," Rhonda said. "She took sixty pills a day just to keep me.

"I had a great childhood. I was involved in everything under the sun—figure skating and ballet and Camp Fire Girls—very social."

As a child, her skating partner was David Santee, who went on to become an Olympic skater. She remembers rehearsing with him carrying her around the ice above his head.

"I weighed ninety pounds then," she said, smiling.

Her parents paid one hundred dollars an hour, the rental rate for a patch of ice. She and her partner rehearsed on that patch. Her "patch time" was eventually moved to 3:00 A.M., the only hour she could secure. A sport she had entered purely for recreation became very competitive, she said, with an ugly spirit shown by jealous and pushy parents.

So Rhonda quit. She said she is delighted when she sees her former skating partner on television, and never wonders how far her career could have gone had she stayed with the sport.

Her mother sold Rhonda's last pair of skates last year.

She played trombone from the time she was in fourth grade through her junior year in college. Trace also plays, but they haven't decided to work up a duet.

In college, she was in Gamma Phi Beta, and fell in love with doing public relations for the sorority, a task that let her practice her major field of study. Her other major was marketing.

Upon graduation, she worked for the Arthur Anderson public relations firm and earned $35,000 a year, not a bad starting salary in the middle 1980s for someone with an undergraduate degree in journalism.

She later did internal public relations for a large trade association and was working on a trade show whose entertainment was singer Randy Travis. She met someone at the show who offered to help her network and find a job if she wanted to move to Nashville. She said she had an immediate fascination for show business and wanted to apply her public relations experience there.

She went to Nashville and was advised by Evelyn Shriver to return to Chicago. She was told her salary would be less than half of what it was in Chicago, and that people in the music business were crazy, Rhonda said.

That gave Rhonda more incentive to make the move.

Her first job paid sixteen thousand dollars less than she had been earning in Chicago, and included inferior benefits.

Her parents were confounded by what she was doing with her life, but paid her Nashville rent nonetheless. Eventually, she began to see socially the guy she had met at the trade show.

She knew that he was divorced and some years older. She didn't know that he once had had a drug and alcohol problem. Someone later burglarized and ransacked her apartment. It turned out that her friend's demons had returned, and her burglar was the guy who had so nicely ushered her into Nashville.

She filed a complaint, never dreaming that the culprit was her friend. After his arrest, she conferred with a judge to have the man committed for drug and alcohol treatment. The man later thanked her for having saved his life, and they remain friends to this day. That marked the end of Nashville boy-girl relationship number one.

After getting her job at Arista, Rhonda expanded on the idea of marketing a dance version of "Boot Scoot Boogie," a major hit for Brooks & Dunn. During that same span she got the idea for a television special in connection with the "Mama's Hungry Eyes" project, an album composed of Merle Haggard songs sung by various artists. Proceeds went to help the needy.

Rhonda became totally absorbed in the music business and was especially supportive of new artists. She cheered on many emerging young singers, whether or not they were on her label. She even dated a then-unknown John Michael Montgomery, as well as actor John Schneider, who was also trying for a hit song.

The relationships mentioned above, including Trace, came after a five-year romance with a guy in college whom Rhonda had believed she would marry. She had dreams of the good life, complete with the figurative white picket fence in suburbia.

Her beau astonished her one day by announcing that he wanted her to move with him to the wilds of Alaska and live amid the mountains and wild animals. She couldn't see herself sleeping to the howls of wolves, or bundling against temperatures that were thirty degrees below zero. Leaving that man, her first love, made her physically sick. She lost fifteen pounds.

Trace's shooting by his second wife did not traumatize him as much as it might have other men. Rhonda thinks that's because her husband is no stranger to hard times.

She pointed out that before meeting her, Trace nearly died in two car accidents, having lost his nose in one (it was sewn back in place). He almost lost his legs to a bulldozer, and got through a hurricane while trapped on an offshore oil rig. He completely cut off his little finger; then, against a doctor's wishes, had it sewn back in a bent position so he could make guitar chords.

Rhonda said that she guessed she and Trace had a history of hard times but, she added, she never even thinks about that.

2

I met Lisa Hartman Black at a celebrity softball game in Nashville not long after her 1991 marriage to Clint. She and I soon became telephone pals and were forever planning lunches that never came off. She travels with Clint, as I do with George. George and Clint never seem to be in Nashville at the same time.

Our telephone friendship grew after Clint and Lisa bought a second home in the Nashville area. They have another place in California. She wanted my recommendations for interior decorators and remodelers. Nashville celebrities are often victimized by contractors who charge inflated prices to stars. I tried to help Lisa avoid that.

I had been a regular viewer of Knots Landing, the television dramatic series in which Lisa was a star in the role of Ciji Dunne during the 1980s. She blended magnificently with Michele Lee, Joan Van Ark, and Donna Mills. The show was a spin-off of Dallas, and I think everyone was intrigued by Lisa's character.

She is, of course, still the star in many prime-time television movies and is one of only a handful of network television's true celebrities to move to Nashville and become a Nashville wife. I wanted to do a chapter about a

Nashville celebrity who is married to a Nashville celebrity. I found out the following.

＊ ＊ ＊

It had been a typical L.A. December day. The afternoon high was in the upper forties, the nighttime low didn't dip below freezing. People rarely see a white Christmas in Los Angeles, California. Clint and Lisa Hartman Black were having dinner after she had coincidentally mentioned, a few days earlier, that she would love to see snow fall during the Yuletide season. She thinks she may have mentioned it twice.

On the drive home, Clint began singing the holiday classic "Let It Snow."

Lisa gave it little thought.

"Then I noticed he was singing it all wrong," she recalled, "and I wondered, How does he not know this song?"

Clint grew up with music and is one of Nashville's most popular singing sensations. He and Garth Brooks burst into the public arena during the same week in 1989. Clint's first song went to number one.

How could someone so musical not know that song? Lisa wondered again.

They left the restaurant, and Clint resumed his strange rendition. Lisa corrected him. They scaled the driveway to their house. For an instant she probably wondered if she was at the wrong address, or suffering from déjà vu.

The entire house, under a cloudless sky, was covered with snow. So was the yard.

Clint had secretly hired a snow production company to come to their dwelling and drench the place in the white stuff. It was the same snow that is sprayed on mountain slopes for skiers.

Clint and Lisa basked in nature's man-made carpet. They made snowmen and angel silhouettes, and rolled around in the snow for hours. It lasted for three days, during which time motorists passed and honked and yelled endorsements for Nashville's coolest couple locked into the heat of high school love. And Clint hadn't even gone beyond the eleventh grade.

Clint's romantic gesture was one of hundreds toward his wife of seven years in a marriage that the press predicted would never last. Reporters called Clint a Nashville guy gone Hollywood through the seduction of a worldly-wise woman.

One writer even called Lisa "Nashville's Robin Givens," implying that she and her mother were trying to abuse Clint's financial affairs the way Ms. Givens and her mother allegedly monopolized the monetary undertakings of Mike Tyson.

Aware of the comparison, Lisa said it hurt her deeply. She doesn't remember who wrote the article or know his whereabouts, but she knows exactly where the husband is whose presence many predicted would be temporary. He's by her side.

"I've never been involved in the business part of his career," Lisa said, defending the implication that she married for money. "When Clint and I got together, he was not happy [with his management]. He had a lot of questions that were not being answered, about his money, about his touring, about his records, about his relationship with RCA. He could not get an answer to any aspect of his career and financial life, pure and simple, and he started to wonder about that. Now this was going on when we met. Our relationship, as I told you, was that we started dating as friends. We neither of us are ones to spill our guts about our private lives."

Lisa said it cost Clint a small fortune in legal fees to get out of an old management contract, and *she* subsidized *him*. Lisa owned a small house in California where Clint lived with her while he studied the legal process with an eye toward severing a contractual arrangement.

He did not defer entirely to his lawyer's judgment, but instead demanded that the lawyer handlead him through the legal process. Clint got out of his contract while getting a legal education.

That made Lisa proud.

Lisa also took issue with the rumors that her mother, Jonni, a professional publicist, handles Clint's publicity.

She said her mother is a workaholic who has always joked that when her time comes to go she wants to die at her desk. All she does for Clint and Lisa is handle the personal details—keep the calendar, respond to personal requests, make sure the house is looked after while they are travelling, etc.

In seven years, the couple has been separated

only a few times, and never longer than a month. When they're apart, Clint calls and sends flowers, often many times daily. When they're together, they talk.

"Of course we have sex," she told a reporter, "but we usually fall asleep just talking. He's a great communicator, and we communicate constantly."

The 1990s Hollywood actress has a blissful romance straight out of a 1940s Hollywood movie. Her impressive career credits indisputably indicate her obsession with her profession, but Lisa Hartman Black found her truest top billing not at a movie studio, but at a marriage altar.

The role of wife is her favorite.

Clint and Lisa eat, sleep, and breathe as one. They're soulmates with a capital S. She waited until the right man came along and was astonished at his arrival. Marriage was not in her master plan. But when she was thirty-five, Clint became the first and last husband she'll ever have.

Show business marriages rarely work when both members are in the business. How has this Nashville wife managed to balance his and her careers and their combined lives?

It takes two, of course, to make a marriage work. And I have a theory about how Lisa does her part. She's a mixture of romance and adaptability.

She's been moving, often chasing a dream, since she was a little girl.

She was in kindergarten when *West Side Story* became her favorite movie. She remembers that the story line moved her to tears. She went into her Houston backyard and acted out the entire plot as a cast of one. She knew every song in the film from having played the soundtrack over and over. (She and Clint were both raised in Houston but did not know each other as youngsters.)

At age six, a star was being conceived inside the perimeters of her parents' modest lot. She would be born when Lisa moved to Hollywood at age nineteen and landed the title role in *Tabitha*, a network spin-off from the 1960s television classic *Bewitched*.

Lisa had graduated from the Houston High School for the Performing Arts after having moved frequently while growing up.

"I went to a different school every year," she said, adding that the movement probably helped prepare her for near nonstop mobility as the wife of a touring entertainer.

Yet she believes her childhood was "normal" because her parents strove to make it so. There were barbecue dinners and outdoor cooking, along with family gatherings at holidays. There was also a heavy emphasis on morality, and Lisa always felt a strong sense of home in whatever house she occupied.

She tried New York City for one year after high school, but to no avail. Then for her career it was off to Hollywood, where she knew only one person. Almost immediately everyone knew her as Tabitha.

"Any idea as to why you were so fortunate so early in your career?" Tom asked.

"I think it's because I studied [acting] all of my

life," she answered. "I was interested from the very beginning and I always took drama classes after school. I studied and I studied and I was very serious about it."

She remembers her audition for the network show from which she made her first national impression as an actress. Many girls had tried for the part.

"It came down to Pam Dawber and me," she said. "And we were sitting opposite each other at the big, huge entry of ABC."

"I've often joked in hindsight that Pam got the hit with *Mork and Mindy* and I got the stiff. Because unfortunately *Tabitha* had a short life.

"We shot thirteen episodes," she said, "and I think the show was a bit dated." Viewers soon didn't care about Tabitha, the daughter of Samantha, a friendly witch. They preferred to turn their channels to *Charlie's Angels, Three's Company,* and all the "jiggle" shows that Lisa said killed hers. The "jiggle" shows featured curvaceous women in tight attire.

So Lisa's producers countered.

"We started changing the *Tabitha* shows, and we wrote some of the scripts to make my character a little more flirtatious," she said. "They didn't take my bra off or anything, but they did try to spice it up a little."

"Were you disenchanted when the show was canceled after thirteen episodes?" she was asked.

"Yeah," she said. "But the good thing was that they signed me to Columbia Pictures. I've always believed that when God closes one door He opens another."

By 1985, the year before she left *Knots Landing*, she would be named Female Star of the '80s by the Hollywood Press Club.

"Do you think you had too much success too early?" Tom asked. "Were you, at twenty, emotionally ready for the fame?"

Without hesitation, she said she was emotionally ready for it.

She attributed her maturity to the values instilled in her as a child and said she can remember the first time the general public gave her the star treatment. She had gone to the Golden Globe Awards and emerged from a limousine to a cheering mob of teenage girls yelling "Tabitha!"

"I remember the feeling of my heart jumping out of my chest," she said. She was torn between her respect for security personnel trying to manipulate the crowd and her desire to sign autographs for all who asked.

"It was one of the sweetest memories I have because it was overwhelming," she said. "I wanted to do the right thing—I wanted to sign all of the autographs—and the cops wouldn't let me. And my heart was pounding and I just kept realizing all of these different emotions."

She talked about the difficulty for women, compared to men, of making it in Hollywood. She said that's largely due to better parts being written for men, and not so much the shop-worn rumor about starlets having to sleep with producers in order to get roles.

"Unfortunately there is some truth to both men and women using their sexuality to further their careers. I personally can't imagine having to do that in order to get work and it's not exclusive to the entertainment industry."

Lisa said she was sexually propositioned only once, by a producer who apparently wasn't overly bright. He hit on her after she had already gotten the part.

She thoroughly researches her roles, and did her most extensive research for the television miniseries *Valley of the Dolls* by not doing research. She refused to see the movie.

She wanted to approach the role of Neely O'Hara without the preconceptions of another actress's interpretation.

Not so for the role of Jade O'Keefe, a prostitute, in a made-for-TV movie.

Lisa interviewed hookers and a transsexual, and hung out with that ilk. She adopted their mannerisms and attitudes in her mind, but felt sorry for them in her heart. She actually met one woman who was selling her body in order to pay her bills and support her children. That gave Lisa emotional overload, and some critics thought that might have made her wrong for the part. She wasn't hardened enough.

She realizes that her opinion of her performance is insignificant when compared to the thinking of the networks or producers who are paying her fee. If they think she's wrong, and if they cancel her character, she doesn't take it personally. It's merely a matter of two differing opinions, not one inferior performance, she feels.

Lisa's most famous role came in *Knots Landing*, as determined by the harshest critics of all—the public. She had done about half of the season when her character was killed. Lisa was pleased with that, as she had already decided to devote more time to the pursuit of a recording career.

But viewers wanted her return, and writers were faced with the challenge of writing a dead character back into the script. She was reluctant to try the revival, but did, and her reprise was an overwhelming hit.

Lisa Hartman Black, in any role, is likable. More important, she's believable.

"Do you think the general public has any idea how hard it is to do a television series?" Tom asked.

"I didn't, and I'm an actress," was her instant reply. "To this day I don't want to do a series like Tom Selleck did in *Magnum, P.I.*, where he was in almost every scene. He was filming six days a week starting at 6:30 A.M."

Filming was preceded by a makeup call.

"When I'm in a movie, I'm in almost every scene," she said, citing how exhausting her production schedule was. "But I do it for four weeks. People doing a weekly series and movies are at it nine or ten months out of the year."

That life, she said, is no life at all.

As of this writing in April 1998, Lisa was looking for a role in an ensemble—that is, she wanted to be part of a large cast such as that on television's immensely popular *ER*.

She could shoot her parts in just two days a week, she estimated.

She was the only woman in an otherwise all-male cast in 1991 in *The Return of Eliot Ness*. She was filming in Canada and felt no discrimination from the men. She said that Robert Stack, the show's star, was a true gentleman. And there was another gentleman on the set. He had four days off from his tiring schedule of one-night performances. Coincidentally, they were the same days that she was excused from production.

So she was delighted when Clint visited her on the set. Their time together only intensified the pace of falling in love.

They had met earlier, during the first hour of 1991, in Houston, where Lisa and her mother attended Clint's New Year's Eve show. He'd never seen *Knots Landing,* and was introduced to Lisa when she and her mother, Jonni, were the first to come backstage after the show. About one hundred fans reportedly stood in line for autographs, and Lisa and Jonni waited through the laborious signings. The first two to arrive became the last two to leave.

Clint was tired from a series of shows and was preoccupied with an album he was preparing to record. But, he said, he left the arena that night and took Lisa's eyes with him.

Lisa recalls the night in detail, adding that there was noise and confusion all around. Nonetheless, she didn't hear much. She said it was as if she and Clint were secretly locked in an invisible cocoon.

Two weeks later, Clint showed up in Los Angeles to do a talk show. He asked legendary show business manager Stan Moress for Lisa's telephone number, and got it. He arrived for their first date in a rented Porsche.

They dined on the beach at Malibu and watched the sun set into the Pacific Ocean.

Love was being born. Early vital signs were perfect.

Clint had said he would not even think about getting married until he was thirty. When he visited Lisa in Toronto on the set of *Eliot Ness*, he was twenty-nine and a half. That, he said, was close enough.

After their Canadian rendezvous, Clint went back on the road with a cast and crew of seventy. A few days later, the number was raised to seventy-one. Three weeks later, Clint played Salt Lake City, Utah. In the space of days they had made a decision for a lifetime commitment. They've officially been a couple ever since.

The two were walking among the shadows of the old buildings on the historic University of Utah campus. There was probably small talk about their beauty, history, and what it would be like to go to college. A few harmless questions were raised, and then Clint posed another.

He asked Lisa to marry him.

On October 20, 1991, a week after the conclusion of Clint's summer tour, he and Lisa became man and wife on a small farm about an hour's drive from

Houston. Family members were the only guests.

Those were Lisa's mother and father; her older sister, Terri (matron of honor); and Terri's husband and her two children. Clint's father was best man, and Clint was also accompanied by his mother, three older brothers, and their wives and children.

The wedding was held outdoors, and Lisa wore an off-the-shoulder, off-white gown. Clint wore a tuxedo jacket, black tie, and black trousers—jeans.

Part of him still had to be a cowboy. Weeks earlier, during a visit on the old *Nashville Now* television show, he had told host Ralph Emery that jeans manufacturers sent him more jeans than he could wear. He pointed out the irony of receiving all of the free attire when he could at last afford to buy as many clothes as he wanted.

Wedding music sifted through the open air before Clint and Lisa took their vows. The only instrument was a harp.

Clint writes, or at least cowrites, his own songs. And he wrote their wedding vows. As stillness settled on a Texas fall afternoon, he said, "Our two lives will become one life. Together, the two of us will overcome what would overcome one."

They left the Texas prairie for the skyscrapers of New York City, where they honeymooned for a week. They discovered that the same sun that had set into the Pacific Ocean rose beautifully from the East River.

"You've got this picture-perfect marriage, yet you were engaged only ten months. Would you recommend such a brief courtship to others?" Tom asked.

"I wouldn't," she snapped. "But it certainly worked for us. There is that old saying about when it's right, you know it. I never would have believed it."

Only their animals share their private lives. They don't have many intimate friends. There isn't a shortage of people, only a shortage of time. Clint and Lisa have little time for others if they can't be together. There are no boys' or girls' nights out in this marriage.

Divorce, in this day and time, is an epidemic, Tom noted. "So why is your marriage so happy?"

"We're best friends," she said. "We never let anything come between us. I know that Clint would never hurt anyone, and he knows that about me. What I'm leading up to is that if something happens that hurts my feelings, I say to him, 'You know, when you said what you did, it hurt my feelings.' And he'll say, 'Oh, here's what was going on.'"

She insisted that Clint is the only man she has ever met who never loses his temper. Never.

She referred to the publicized battle he underwent to get out of his management agreement. The stress on him showed, and he could have been expected to take it out on her, she said. But he never did. Not once, not during days of pressurized litigation.

"He had every right to be short with me, to lose it, and then say 'I'm sorry,'" she said. "But he never did. It never happened. I don't know where that comes from. He's that way with his employees and on the road. He just never gets angry."

Not long after Clint and Lisa were married, he was sued by a woman who claimed he was the father of her child. A paternity suit. Now that *had* to be damaging to the marriage that was portrayed on the cover of *People* magazine as a couple dancing among rose petals.

When asked about this, Lisa says she cannot talk about it for legal reasons, but that it is no longer an issue to either party.

Clint may be the last man in Lisa's life, but he isn't the first. She lived with actor Barry Bostwick and underwent a publicized breakup in 1984.

"Was that painful for you?"

"It was a positive relationship and it ended on a positive note. The fact that it was publicized didn't make a difference either way. I believe that the way I was raised has everything to do with the way I react to things of that nature."

She could not have been prepared for what would happen years later when she fell in love with Clint. "I was never looking for a man to marry, or even the whole 'rest of my life' premise. Not because I was driven by my work, but because I just wasn't looking for that."

She said that by the time she met Clint and astonished herself with her willingness to marry him, she realized she had pretty much done all of the things she had wanted to do.

Marriage was the next logical step.

Clint has recorded hit songs with Wynonna, Martina McBride, and Roy Rogers. Clint joined a half-dozen other artists to sing on George's 1992 hit, "Rockin' Chair." He became a member of the Grand Ole Opry in 1991 and has partaken in cast sing-alongs on national television. Lisa herself is a singer who has recorded albums. Yet the man who has recorded with so many hasn't recorded with the wife he loves so much.

Does that bother her?

"No," she said. "I do a good job [singing], but I live with an incredible voice and I've learned more in the past six or seven years what that really means."

She has no resentment toward the women who do record with Clint, and no aspirations to record with him herself. Yet she included him in her acting career.

In early 1998, the two finished filming *Cadillac Jack and Ponder*, the story of a rodeo cowboy who was wrongfully convicted of murder. The show was scheduled to air later in the year. Clint was the star, Lisa was his costar. Clint had done brief stints on television's *Wings* and the motion picture *Maverick*. But this was his first starring role.

The project was three years in development. Lisa said it was taken to network officials, who said that the obvious cast for costar was her. Why not have a real-life husband and wife portray a real-life husband and wife?

Clint and Lisa slept, ate, rehearsed, and acted together for nineteen consecutive days. That's 456 hours without being apart. Clint told a national magazine that he could have gone on indefinitely with the work as long as Lisa was working with him.

I began to wonder if this was romance or emotional codependency. I don't know if these two need to make more love or enter a twelve-step program. I wondered if they should go back to bed or to an analyst's couch.

But my curiosity doesn't matter. Nothing matters to Lisa and Clint except Lisa and Clint—not much, anyhow.

"When one speaks, the other listens raptly," described an article in the April 1994 issue of *Good Housekeeping* magazine. "Often when they're talking to a third party, they're still looking into each other's eyes, as if a blink might interrupt some shared telepathy. They speak of love and marriage with the fervor of newlyweds."

In many interviews, Clint has stressed Lisa's domestic side. A woman who's had many hit television series, does at least two prime-time shows annually, and has played the parts of worldly women has no reservations about washing dishes by hand.

She said that she surprised herself with her eagerness to wait on Clint. It's a side of her she hadn't seen until their marriage. The whole thing sounds more like a conversion than a marriage. But they say love changes all.

She and Clint had their own bus, and she reportedly cooked for him on the bus range and oven. But not anymore. That's because they travel by private jet.

She said that air travel allows them more time to address business affairs. When still on a bus, they arrived at a show in time to perform it, then had to rush off for another venue. Despite the expense of leasing a jet, the extra time it allows makes it cost effective, Lisa said.

I was dying to know if they were members of the "mile-high club," but didn't ask.

I wondered why the relationship didn't suffer from overexposure. Lisa said that she and Clint simply never get tired of each other. Familiarity does not breed contempt.

"We never feel the need for space," she said. "I don't think there's anything wrong with people needing space, but we don't need it."

She doesn't talk like hers is textbook happiness. Textbooks are nonfiction. The relationship she describes is straight out of a romance novel. And nothing makes her hedge on her description of bliss. God may have created Heaven and Earth in seven days for the rest of us, but He took an obvious eighth to make a special world for Clint and Lisa, she'd have us believe.

As I replayed her tape-recorded conversation, I could find no reason to doubt this yarn of modern Nirvana. I mean, Clint does things that would make most women misty. For example:

Lisa was doing the *Late Late Show with Tom Snyder* in 1997 and talking all about herself and her career, which is why one does that show. The CBS network allows an 800 number for viewers who want to ask questions of Snyder's celebrity guests.

Lisa had two callers. One was Clint. How'd he get through? He must have pulled a lot of strings to get around the thousands of other viewers who are put on hold nightly.

"Hi, honey," Lisa said, at the sound of Clint's amplified voice. Snyder seemed taken aback. I doubt that a famous woman's husband had ever previously called her on his program.

Lisa seemed delighted but not at all surprised. Why wouldn't Clint interrupt six million viewers to tell his wife he loved her? Ho-hum.

In January 1998, Clint appeared on *The Oprah Winfrey Show*. Of course, he sang. There, in the front row, sat Oprah. There, next to Oprah, sat Lisa. Clint and Lisa came as a set.

Lisa was filming a movie on one of those rare occasions when Clint had to be in another city. She rehearsed her scene with her costar. They did a walk-through, and everybody was comfortable. The costar was supposed to speak a line, walk through a door, and she was to meet him with her own line.

No problem.

"Quiet on the set!" the director commanded. "And action!"

The costar said his line through the door. Lisa thought his voice sounded strange, but remained in character, as the cameras were rolling. The costar burst through the door.

It wasn't the costar at all. It was Clint.

The entire cast and crew had been in on the

romantic hoax. They knew that Clint had flown a thousand miles to surprise the wife he had not seen for two days.

The mere sight of him threw her into tears.

"Of course I cried," she said. "Oh . . . it was so wonderful."

3

I first met Mrs. Kix (Barbara) Brooks during a press conference for Soul Mates, the Nashville Network show that profiles the wives of country music stars. In many ways, it's the television equivalent to this book, except it's more shallow.

Barbara is one of the brightest of all of the Nashville wives, given her academic and entrepreneurial background. As of this writing, I last saw her at George's birthday party in September 1997. I was glad she accepted my invitation to attend.

Barbara Brooks did not break up anyone's marriage, did not nurture her husband through drug or alcohol treatment, has never been the victim of domestic violence, did finish high school, did graduate from college, has a graduate degree, does not believe her husband has ever been unfaithful, and has no live-in cook or nanny.

Believe it or not, she's a Nashville wife.

Her husband is the energetic member of Brooks & Dunn, whose recordings are now the second highest-selling in the history of vocal duos. (Simon and Garfunkel are first.)

Barbara isn't even from the South.

"I'm from outside of Boston," she said. "I grew up in a little town founded in 1633. There was history everywhere you looked. Our house was 150 years old."

Her childhood passion was sailing on the Atlantic Ocean with her parents and sister. She had her own sailboat by age ten.

During the summers, her mother dropped her off at a yacht club each morning, and she spent many entire days alternately navigating her boat within the harbor and diving off the pier.

Barbara's dad, now retired, was a naval architect and marine engineer whose professional life was spent working for Bethlehem Steel. He built huge oceangoing freighters and tankers. Closest to his heart, though, was the 1938 wooden sailboat he bought in the early 1960s. The entire family worked together to refit and refurbish the boat. Barbara's mom sewed bunk mattress covers and repaired sails. Barbara and her sister, Mardi, learned early to sand, caulk, paint, and varnish. Her dad did everything from rebuilding the diesel engine and bilge pumps to building a collapsible dining table. A lot of the work had to be repeated each year.

Barbara remembers the experience fondly, but with a rueful smile.

"I may not have appreciated it quite as much at the time, but I realize now that working on that boat with my dad did several things—it gave me a chance to spend a lot of time talking with him, giving us a very solid relationship to carry into my teenage years; it gave me a work ethic and taught me how to finish a job; and it taught me basics about a lot of different jobs and my ability to do them. Consequently, I am not at all afraid to pick up and use a hammer, saw, power sander, or fiberglass kit. These are all skills that help me out a lot, especially with a husband who spends as much time on the road as mine does."

She also recalls the joys of sailing and times on the ocean that were more dangerous than she realized as a child.

"But my dad had such a calm and confident demeanor that I didn't necessarily know to be scared," she said. "There were a couple of times when we were out and storms came up and it was pretty intense. He'd strap us on to keep us from going over the side with all the water coming over the bow. I just loved it. I'd ride the boat like a horse. You know how sailboats lean when they sail? I'd get up on the edge and just ride it like a horse—oh yeah, a real Yankee cowgirl."

The allusion to horses is not accidental. Barbara calls herself horse-crazy and says she has been since a very early age. She never owned a horse while growing up since ownership was not within her parents' financial potential. Riding stables were expensive too. But her room was filled with horse models and books and even an old cavalry saddle her dad found at a garage sale.

Her dream was realized in 1993 when Kix gave her a paint mare for Christmas.

"We had traveled down to Louisiana to be with Kix's dad Leon at his farm for Thanksgiving and arrived about 11:00 P.M.," she recalled. We carried the kids in and put them to bed and I had just sat down to relax with his dad when Kix comes in with a flashlight and says, 'Come on, let's go see the longhorns. I want to see my longhorns.' Kix and Ronnie Dunn [Kix's singing partner] had given each other longhorn steers for some reason or another.

"I looked at Leon and rolled my eyes, but trudged on out with Kix. On the way to the pasture, we passed one of the corrals and my light—or more likely Kix's—caught a flash of white. I turned to look and saw a beautiful paint horse. She nickered and came to the fence. I rubbed her nose and asked, 'Where did you come from, who do you belong to?'

" 'Can't you guess?' Kix said.

"I just started bawling," said Barbara.

Barbara was so happy in her role as a horse owner that it didn't matter to her that she fell off that new horse the next day and spent three days in a Louisiana hospital with internal bleeding and a deeply bruised hip.

"Kix and I were on our first ride and when we got to a big open field he said, 'Let's run 'em!' We took off and I quickly discovered that my twenty-year-old riding skills needed some polishing and that my saddle was loose. I lost my right stirrup and the saddle started to slip hard to the left. I pulled back on Angel, but since I was holding the horn with my right hand I must have pulled her to the left, 'cause that's where she went. I made a quick decision to go right and landed hard.

"Kix told me later," she continued, "that the first thought that went through his head when he saw me fall was, Oh my God, she'll lose the baby! That was really odd since I wasn't pregnant. He attributes that thought to all the westerns he watched as a child—the women always lost babies when they fell off horses."

While Barbara was in the hospital, they were taking blood every few hours to see if the internal bleeding had stopped. Barbara soon noticed that she never saw the same technician twice and that a couple of them were really not very good at their job, judging by the huge spreading of bruises on her arms. The head of the department, who turned out to be the father of Nashville recording session drummer Lonnie Wilson, stopped by to apologize. It turned out that the technicians were taking turns, including trainees, because everybody wanted to see the music star's wife!

"That was one of my first experiences with celebrity and it struck me as pretty funny because I was certainly anything but impressive, lying there white as a ghost wearing a hospital johnny.

"When we got back to Nashville," she went on, "and the news circulated around town about my accident, the newspapers and CNN picked it up. Jackie

Onassis and Ashley Judd had fallen from horses the same week and CNN put us together in the same story. I thought that was pretty neat company."

Barbara and Kix today own nine horses and plan to breed performance horses—cutting, roping, and reining horses—on their farm south of Nashville.

Barbara went to Wellesley College, the same all-girls college in Massachusetts that her mother and sister had attended. After earning a bachelor's degree in psychology, she became a research assistant for a National Institute of Mental Health project at the University of Rochester. She had an office among psychology graduate students and professors.

"I decided I never had met a larger group of messed-up people in my life," she said, laughing. "I decided at that point that I wouldn't go after my own doctorate."

The funding for the doctoral project had been cut and Barbara's job in Rochester disappeared with it. She moved to Maine and opened a fabric store and dressmaking operation in an old building. There, a friend owned a yarn store where Barbara had worked during vacations from college.

In Maine, she met her first and only husband when the two were invited to a housewarming party. The hostess had told her that she was dating Kix, but was actually in love with another man. Barbara therefore saw no conflict in accepting a date with Kix.

Kix was working at his sister's advertising agency, writing radio jingles and advertising copy. He holds an undergraduate degree in speech and theater.

Kix, she said, really wanted to try his hand at the music business full-time. He had been playing in clubs and bars in Maine after work and on weekends. He had saved enough money to sustain himself while awaiting an opportunity in New Orleans, a musical haven where he was certain he could find work.

En route, Kix stopped in Nashville to visit a former high-school buddy who had become a music publishing executive. That executive, Jody Williams, now head of MCA Publishing, encouraged Kix to try Nashville and, after the stint in New Orleans, Kix did.

Barbara had visited Kix in New Orleans, and later in Nashville. After Kix opted to stay in Nashville, she did too.

After four years the fabric shop was losing its appeal for Barbara, especially since Kix was gone. Bored with cotton and linen, she decided to move to Nashville and see what would happen with the man with whom she had fallen in love.

But the decision to cohabit was not instant.

Barbara arrived in Nashville in the spring of 1981 in a 1969 Cadillac. That holds no relevance except that the vehicle, a virtual land yacht, was probably useful when Kix hauled his belongings from his Nashville address to what became *their* Nashville address.

"Technically, I moved all of my stuff into his

apartment because I didn't have anywhere else to go," Barbara said. "The day after I got there I found an apartment I would be able to move into in two weeks. When that day came, Kix helped me move all my stuff in his van and my car; then we went out that night. We had to go to two different places to get a jacket. It just seemed so silly. He moved in a couple of days later."

Besides her anniversary of August 1, 1981, another date sticks in her mind. On June 16, 1981, Kix said he thought the two should discontinue living together out of wedlock.

"My stomach headed for the basement," she said. "And then, after a long pause, he asked if I would marry him. I know he planned that all day long—the rat!" she said, laughing.

"Had you been wanting to get married?" Barbara was asked.

"Well, I didn't know that I did," she said. "I kind of figured that if we stayed together, in a couple of years we'd probably get married. That was totally Kix's idea at the moment. He had called my parents, my sister, he had called his dad, he'd called his grandparents. Everybody knew it before I did."

"He called them seeking approval?"

"My parents? He did—yes."

I personally thought that Kix's polling of the family was very gallant. Barbara agreed.

A formal wedding was planned, rehearsed, and executed within six weeks. Barbara said that, given the swiftness, she's sure many people thought she was pregnant.

"I'm sure they did," she affirmed. "But we figured the more time we allowed for preparations, the bigger the production would get, and we wanted it fairly small and to get it over with. Kix's thought was that he would not be able to concentrate on songwriting until we had the wedding behind us and could settle down, so let's get it done! The fact that we didn't have a child for five years after we got married—a lot of people probably got very tired of waiting for that baby."

On July 31, 1981, the night of his bachelor party, Kix extended an invitation to Barbara, her bridesmaids, and other females to attend.

"No naked girls jumped out of a cake," she said of the soiree, which she recalls with amusement.

The women guests systematically and sensibly began to retire in preparation for the big day, but at daylight, Kix and chums went water-skiing and ran out of gasoline.

They were eventually pulled to shore by a fisherman. By late afternoon on her wedding day, no one could find her betrothed, Barbara said.

"I knew he was missing in action," she said.

"Did that make you apprehensive?"

"No, I was a little apprehensive before that," she answered. "Wedding day nerves had started a lot earlier that day."

"You didn't think he would run out on the deal?"

"No, I wasn't really worried about that, and besides his dad would have killed him if he'd done that."

Kix slept all day on the day of his wedding. Then he overslept. He was almost late for his wedding.

Was he rested?

"No, he fell asleep on our wedding night as soon as his head hit the pillow." Barbara laughed.

"Were you angry?" I wanted to know.

"No, I knew I'd get something out of him later."

"Where did you go for your honeymoon?" Tom pressed.

"Lake Tahoe," she said, beaming. "And he was quite rested by the time we got there, thank you."

Barbara was asked how she and Kix have held together a seventeen-year marriage with two children during the pressure of show business during the stress-filled 1990s.

"There is no friction in this marriage," she said. "There really isn't. We have a ball. We're well suited. We agree on most things."

"We've always viewed our marriage as a partnership, as a pairing of equals working toward the same goals. Kix said it very well soon after we got married. A friend of his dad's had offered him a job driving pipeline equipment up to New York State. I was semi-weepy at the thought of him being gone so much for the next few weeks so soon after we had gotten married. Kix said that it didn't matter if we were apart for a few days at a time then because we were going to spend the rest of our lives together. We have always tried not to let the day-to-day stuff get to us and to keep the big picture—our whole lives together—in sight."

Kix had earned a living penning tunes in Nashville while Barbara worked her way up from her first Nashville job at Vanderbilt University for five dollars an hour. Kix struck major pay dirt when he became half of a duo. He hadn't planned that—he had wanted to be a soloist. His accepting a singing partner had to have affected his entire family.

"In light of the fact that Kix had pursued a career as a soloist, did either of you have any regrets about his being packaged in a duo?" Tom asked Barbara.

"I don't think we have any regrets, because it worked out so well," she said. "We had some questions, you know, how was it going to work and were they going to be compatible and was it going to be fun?

"I think they've appreciated being able to share the responsibility and having another person to work with in making major career decisions. And when one of them feels lousy the other can take the interviews that day. I think that looking back they would both say that it's been real positive."

"Do people ever ask you which is Kix and which is Ronnie?" I asked.

"Yes," she said. "I tell them Kix is the cute one. I think Kix is adorable."

"Do the four of you, Mr. and Mrs. Ronnie Dunn and Mr. and Mrs. Kix Brooks, get along?" I asked.

"I think so," Barbara said. "We don't do an awful lot together. The guys are together so much on the road that we have a tendency to hibernate when Kix is home.

"Janine [Mrs. Ronnie Dunn] and I were at such different places in our lives when we first met that we haven't gotten as close as we might have otherwise," Barbara said. "When the Dunns first got to Nashville and the guys got started, Kix and I had been married for ten years. I was working full-time and taking care of two small children. Janine and Ronnie had only been married a few months, his kids were in Oklahoma, and she was coping with the sale of the company she had inherited from her first husband.

"I didn't have a lot of time to show Janine around Nashville or help her meet people. Luckily, Janine is a very friendly, outgoing person and she didn't need me to figure all that out. She found friends to do things with and probably learned a lot more quickly than I did where to shop and where to eat.

"Both of our lives have changed, but they sure haven't gotten any less busy. As silly as it sounds for two people living as close as we do, our friendship is more based on phone calls than actually being together. We talk pretty frequently and those calls often last quite a while, or as long as they can last with her four-year-old and my older, but still demanding, interrupters."

Tom asked Barbara the question Nashville wives hear most frequently: "Do you worry about your husband being unfaithful while he's touring?"

"No," she said very decisively.

"Why? He's a good-looking guy."

"Yes, he is, but he's also a very honorable person," she said. "I don't think it [adultery] is in his personality. Besides that, he doesn't have time. He works too hard when he's out there."

Kix has his own bus, and Barbara and their children ride with him from show to show during summer months when school is not in session.

She said she has therefore seen firsthand how hard Kix works while on tour, and how his days are filled with so much more than merely rehearsing and performing. She specifically cited the immense number of interviews and the unprecedented press attention focused on country music in the wake of its explosive popularity.

She said today's modern stars are busy overseeing auxiliary businesses, such as merchandising and endorsements, which were not a big part of the country music industry a few years ago. There is no time to waste sleeping off hangovers from the previous night's party, as was the case with their predecessors.

Also, she doesn't believe that modern record labels would tolerate that kind of behavior for very long. With all the media attention, reports of any misbehavior would get around quickly. Barbara goes on to mention the fact that there are several artists around Nashville who have lost their recording deals because they weren't taking care of business.

George lived wastefully when his career was young. He'd do a show, get drunk, stay up all night, sleep all day on his bus, then do another show and get drunk the next night. His cronies lived the same way. They got so wasted, they'd have to ask each other if they'd had a good time the previous night.

She said that she has seen little change in Kix in the wake of his celebrity, except for a greater commitment to taking care of his health. She laughed about his relaxed demeanor as evidenced by his ability to go to sleep practically at will. She said he can lie down and doze soundly before a show, knowing that when he awakens he'll face thousands of screaming fans.

"What if Brooks & Dunn had never happened?" she was asked. "What would have become of Kix and Barbara Brooks?"

"He would have continued as a songwriter," she said. "He might have moved more into the business end of the music business because he has such a good head for that as well. He was writing at Tree Publishing, and he might have gone into songwriter relations or production. I mean, I was happy then and I'm happy now."

"What do you think is different about raising kids in a celebrity home and lifestyle?" Barbara was asked.

"I can only talk about our kids and lifestyle," she said. "I think there are a few differences—good and bad. Different people might have different opinions about which ones are good and which are bad. Most kids don't get to wave at the tour buses that stop in front of their house. Most kids don't get their pictures in national magazines. Most kids don't get to go to the Grammy Awards ceremony in New York City or meet Michael Jordan in the Chicago Bulls locker room. Most kids don't get literally pushed out of the way by someone wanting to meet their dad. Most don't have to wonder if their new friend only wants to be their friend because of who their dad is."

"What do you cite as one of your most romantic recollections of this relationship?"

"You mean, besides my horse? Well, we think the same thing a lot of the time," she said. "We have the same thoughts running through our heads at the same time. He'll look at me and say just what I'm thinking.

"And he's got a song," she continued. "The kids are going to take offense at this, but there's a song he wrote called 'Alone Again.' It's about what a couple went through to be alone again. It starts when they [the couple in the song] go to a party and they leave to be alone again. They get married in front of all of those people, and they go and they're alone again. Then they have their little kids and the kids grow up and it is, 'See what we went through to be alone again.' It's a wonderful song.

"One day, soon after Brooks & Dunn had started and Kix was gone, roses arrived at the door for no special occasion and all Kix had put on the card was 'Alone Again.' I knew what that meant."

Barbara's day begins at 6:30 A.M. when she gets the kids up and starts the coffee. Kix comes to breakfast at 7:15 A.M., she said, because he wants to see his children before they go to school during his limited time at home.

Their kids attend public schools because she thinks private schools encourage snobbery, and Kix wants them to be with a larger, more diverse group of people.

Her chat for this book was fast coming to an end, as her "hands-on" policy of household management was calling. Workmen were making another room in the basement, and Barbara was overseeing their progress. Later, she said, she would do a few loads of laundry before getting ready for George's birthday party.

"People are always asking if I've tried a new restaurant, and they think I'm kidding when I tell them no, that we don't get out much," she said. "What can I say? I think we have a pretty normal life."

4

I first met Sandy Brooks backstage at one of the country music award shows. Garth, her husband, had only begun what would become the most successful career in country music history. A few years later, Garth and Sandy happened to sit behind George and me when George was inducted into the Country Music Hall of Fame during a network television show. A television camera picked up Garth's face, streaked with tears. They were tears of pride and joy on George's behalf. Neither George nor I will ever forget his sensitivity and gratitude. I have never been anywhere where Sandy was in attendance when she didn't make a point to look me up to say hello. Many young Nashville wives, whose husbands have had only a fraction of Garth's success, feel too big to acknowledge the veteran entertainers or their spouses. Sandy Brooks never strayed from the roots of her rearing, obviously planted firmly in respect for her mentors. Country music is a better business because of Garth. I'm a better person for knowing Sandy.

* * *

There were ten rows of pews that held eighty-five parishioners in the former Good Shepherd United Methodist Church at 1921 Gallatin Road North in Madison, Tennessee. There was a handmade altar colored with wood stain and spotted with worshipers' tears. With paint as their only finish, the walls were no more than colored concrete blocks. One held a sign that told how many people had attended Sunday School the previous week, and how much money was put into the offering plates.

THE BEST IS YET TO BE read a homemade sign in the yard.

It was a humble place, destroyed to make room for a men's store. Designer suits now hang where people prayed on Sundays and Wednesdays, and Mrs. Garth (Sandy) Brooks cleaned by hand on Fridays and Saturdays, working alone in the small and silent sanctuary.

In her early Nashville days, there was more to Sandy's life than custodial labor. She also toiled eight hours a day trimming, bunching, and selling roses inside a flower shop. And she sold boots, with her husband, at a boot store where they were the sole employees.

Sandy Brooks worked three jobs while hoping her husband might have one spectacular career. And he did. Garth became, quite simply, the most popular entertainer in the world.

Sandy's role was and is so important, so pivotal, that she can't be called the woman behind the man. She is the woman beside the man: their spirits are entwined. He knows that, in the formative days, he couldn't have launched toward superstardom without her. In fact, he wouldn't have even tried.

"The first time he went to Nashville [in 1985] he stayed for twenty-three hours," Sandy said. She had helped him pack for the drive, and he set out by himself on a journey where the most significant event was a flat tire. His spirits were soon as deflated.

"He came home. Within four months we were engaged and then married seven months later, on May 24, 1986. He worked in clubs for about a year, maybe a year and a half, and we agreed he had to go back to Nashville—to try it again. So in May of 1987 I quit college. We packed up everything we had in a U-Haul, with our $1,500 savings, and each other. I knew that if he didn't try it, he'd spend the rest of his life wondering what would have happened if he had. And I knew he'd never be happy, always wondering what might have been."

Sandy Gail Brooks was born on January 16, 1965, to John and Pat Mahl. She and her older sister, Debbie, were raised in a modest house in Owasso, Oklahoma, a city of about five thousand, situated ten miles north of Tulsa.

"Our house was like Old McDonald's farm," explained Pat. "We had all kinds of animals, and Sandy had to take care of them. Both of our girls had to do chores at home, and Sandy always seemed to want to do the ones that were outdoors."

And Sandy's parents supported her in whatever she did. Her parents didn't simply take her and Debbie to church. They accompanied them. Sandy was a cheerleader, and her parents went to every game she cheered. She was involved in the Future Farmers of America (FFA), played basketball, and ran track, and did all of it of her own will—with her family's support, of course.

Sandy didn't know Garth then. Neither did she know that they had been born in the same city in the same hospital on the same floor. Sandy and Garth together make me consider destiny.

Sandy makes me consider miracles. Her parents had tried unsuccessfully to have a second child after Debbie. Her mother had lost two babies. She and Debbie prayed for another baby. Then Sandy came along, and Pat was convinced it was a miracle. And it was as if Sandy had divine protection, as evidenced by three concussions she suffered as a result of her high-energy behavior. At the age of six, she fell from an elephant slide twenty feet onto concrete and lay unconscious in her mother's arms for eight hours, and she was once thrown head-first over the handlebars of a motorcycle without a helmet. Maybe it's a miracle she's alive today.

Her zest for life was manifested through an impish, but harmless, spirit. And she was without fear. She had no reservations, for example, about biting her sister, Debbie, who was older and taller. She loved to play tricks on her sister.

"She wasn't one bit afraid of Debbie," her

mother laughed, "or anybody or anything." Sandy's mother calls her a tomboy in the same breath she calls her a miracle baby.

I never cease to be amazed at all the rumors and published misinformation about how the Nashville wives met their husbands. The press seems to love to sensationalize it.

Sandy is a refreshingly honest person who freely admits that she didn't immediately lose her heart to Garth. She lost her fist.

After graduating from high school in May 1983, she spent her freshman year in college at Oklahoma State University as if at a perpetual party. She was away from home for the first time, and she was spreading her wings, soaring into the orbit of good times.

In 1984, she was in the ladies' room at the Tumbleweeds Club in Stillwater, Oklahoma. A woman came into the room and began to argue with Sandy about an old boyfriend. Sandy insisted she was no longer interested in the guy, told the girl she was free to date him, and asked her to stop calling her at all hours and harassing her.

The girl said something smart, and Sandy asked her once more to leave her alone. More aggression from the woman. Sandy then told her for a final time.

"And I said, 'If you don't leave me alone I'm just going to have to hurt you,' and at that point in time I raised back my fist and I meant to put it right next to her, you know, around her head, and I said to leave me the blank alone," Sandy explained. "And my fist went through the wall because the wall was nothing, just paneling."

Sandy's hand was stuck. The club bouncer had to come into the women's room to get it out. His name was Garth. How many women do you know who are spirited enough to get into such a situation, and honest enough to tell about it? I've heard only a handful admit to a barroom fight. Sandy's the first to confess to a bathroom fight.

Imagine the scene. There was probably even some laughter. She had her fist in the wall, he had his hands on her fist, they had their eyes locked together. I wonder how Shakespeare would have recorded that.

Garth told her she was unable to drive, and suggested she wait at the club until he got off work. Soon after they left the Tumbleweeds, he suggested she come to his place—for the night.

"Knowing him now, I would say he did not make a pass at me," Sandy said. "But at the time I thought it was a pass because basically he said, 'Look, you can come, you can sleep in my roommate's bunk, I know you'll be safe.'

"Knowing him now, I believe he meant that. But at the time, I had seen him in there plenty of times and he was pretty much of a ladies' man and I said, 'There's no way I'm going home with you.' So he took me to the elevator [at the dormitory] and put me on the elevator and said 'be careful' and that was it."

He called the next morning. Sandy surmises that Garth got her number from someone at the dormitory. His first question: "Why was a nice girl like you in a situation like that?"

Sandy told me she went to college to fulfill a promise to her mother and that she had promised her family she would try it for a year. Before the year was over, Sandy decided she would not graduate but would pursue a career as an X-ray technician.

That was before the return of the ladies' room rescuer. She and Garth saw each other the next day. They walked around the lush campus. Hands joined, they had little idea their hearts would soon be too.

"We walked and talked all day, up until that night, and he's got a song that he wrote about it," she said. "He's never recorded it." Then Sandy, without provocation, began to recite to me the words to a song written for her twelve years ago by an undiscovered singer-songwriter in northeastern Oklahoma. Her eyes took on a faraway stare. She, Tom Carter, and I sat inside her Nashville office, but one of us was long ago and far away.

First impressions are always the most lasting. For Sandy, they were also the most accurate. Her initial day with Garth convinced her that he was an extremely sensitive and caring man. She believes the same thing to this day—only more so.

Sandy may have surprised herself by enrolling for

her sophomore year in college, with her major in sociology, focusing on child abuse and juvenile delinquency. She said she enrolled at Garth's urging. It would turn out to be her last year of college, and there would never be study to become an X-ray technician. She said Garth had to make up some courses to get his undergraduate degree, and he also took some hours toward his master's. Somehow, I got the feeling the couple knew they were going through the motions until Garth returned to Nashville with his companion and bride.

In May 1987, Garth and Sandy arrived in Nashville with a carload of furniture and a dream. They were accompanied by Garth's band, Santa Fe. And they all lived in one house—Sandy, Garth, a married couple and their child, three single men, one cat, and one dog—in one two-bedroom house with three rooms in the basement.

"There were eight of us in this five-bedroom home and it was one hundred and fifty dollars [per bedroom] for rent," Sandy reflected.

"But you were young and in love," Tom noted.

"Young and in love," she said. "And it didn't matter where we were or what we were doing as long as Garth and I were together.

"So we developed a system.

"Jeri [wife of another struggling musician] and I would get the Sunday paper and look through it and see what food was on sale," she remembered. "Then we'd make up menus just like you would have at school—spaghetti and salad and bread on Monday; meat loaf, mashed potatoes, green beans on Tuesday—you get the idea. We'd post the menu on the refrigerator. House members had to sign up for meals," she continued. "If they didn't sign up, they didn't eat. Most everyone ate on Mondays, spaghetti night, when the meals cost only ninety-eight cents each. I know because I did the math. As I look back, I wish I had kept one of the menus from those days. But I didn't think to do that. I didn't think about anything except the next paycheck and how we'd make it another week.

"Everybody thought that it wouldn't work, that Jeri and I wouldn't get along. But actually, it was the men that didn't agree: They had their own ideas about how to do things."

After living in Nashville for two weeks, Garth spotted a classified advertisement for a manager of a boot store. Part of the manager's responsibilities would be to hire one person.

Guess who it was?

"Was Garth easy to work for?"

"Oh yes. I was supposed to work for thirty-two hours a week, but sometimes I didn't," she said. "But I got paid for thirty-two hours."

Garth and Sandy must have moved a lot of boots

through the place. After they quit, the store eventually went out of business.

Garth worked there for two years (until 1989), while Sandy stayed on for a third. That store held a lot of significance for the young couple. Garth had become a paid songwriter (earning $300 a month as an advance against potential royalties), and he had the freedom to cowrite songs during the day while Sandy manned the store. Garth eventually sold boots to James Garver and Steve McClure, two musicians who came in looking for footwear and landed jobs in Garth's band that they hold to this day.

Money was tight, and Sandy was working a lot of hours. In addition to her job at the boot store, Sandy was also laboring at the floral shop and performing custodial duties at the church. Meanwhile, Garth was making his mark. He signed on with Capitol Records and was becoming a successful songwriter. He was concerned about his wife and, after explaining to her that they were financially stable enough, he urged her to quit her floral job. Two months later it happened.

Sandy had been stressed out by Garth's new absenteeism. In the wake of his signing with Capitol Records, he had gone to California to cowrite songs. There were a few performance dates, but nothing like the mass to come. She was stuck in a drafty house where she couldn't sleep one night from worry and the coldness of the room.

"I was too cold to get up and close the window," she said. "I just kept wanting to get under the covers, but I could never get warm, and I kept thinking about him and wondering where he was and what he was doing."

Sandy picked up Garth at the airport. Within twenty-four hours, the entire right side of her face sagged, all the way to her neck. She could not even close her right eye or control her mouth. On the way home from the airport, they had stopped at a restaurant. When she tried to drink through a straw, liquid ran down her chin. She couldn't close her mouth around the plastic tube.

"The next day it kept getting worse," she said. "I'd never heard of Bell's palsy, and I didn't know what was wrong. I was scared to death." She thought about the three concussions she'd suffered in childhood, and feared she had a brain tumor.

"I kept calling Garth at the office, and he kept calling me, and we kept missing each other," she went on. "Meanwhile, it just kept getting worse. He came home that night, and walked in and the first thing he said was, 'What the hell is the matter with your face?' I just started crying. It broke my heart, and I was scared to death. We had no insurance. I had quit the job I had with the only employer who carried health insurance on me just two weeks earlier. Garth was getting his weekly advances, and we had gotten $10,000 as a signing bonus when he was signed to his record deal.

"The lawyers took four thousand of that, and we

paid the medical bills with the remaining six thousand."

The Bell's palsy eventually cleared itself.

This is when it all started getting crazy and the whirlwind of their career started. There are all kinds of official "reasons" for Garth's success. There's the one about him pinch-hitting one night for a singer at the Blue Bird, Nashville's premier listening room, where he was heard by a record executive who had passed on Garth's earlier requests for a deal. Still other Nashville insiders say Garth's biggest break came when the late Joe Harris, the dean of Nashville booking agents, booked Garth for several months before his first record was ever recorded, and Garth gained a word-of-mouth reputation among promoters about his uncanny ability to excite an audience. There are a lot of people, now, who want to claim responsibility for the success of Garth and Sandy Brooks.

Garth's first release, "Much Too Young (To Feel This Damn Old)," came out on March 25, 1989. The song rose to number eight on *Billboard*. Garth's launch was firmly off the pad. Six months later, on September 9, Capitol released "If Tomorrow Never Comes." It shot to number one.

The first significant tour had begun that same year, May 1989. During that tour, Sandy had a misconception about Garth's life on the road, and wrongly assumed that he slept all day, then had a wonderful time performing his music at night.

"I didn't realize that his day began with radio interviews at 7:00 A.M., and then maybe he'd have to do another interview, then an in-store signing at a record store and a bunch of other stuff before he ever did the show that night."

Her resentment compounded, especially when she couldn't reach him by telephone after his shows. She pursued her own nightlife, and there were nights, she said, when her husband couldn't find her at 3:00 A.M. Garth and Sandy, they soon realized, were drifting apart.

"We both made mistakes but realized our problems before it was too late. Our marriage was made stronger by it," she said, "because it was both our faults. I knew nothing of what he was up to on the road, and he knew nothing of what I was up to, and we came together and said, 'This isn't what we had planned for each other,' and we refocused and we realized that we are a team and that we loved each other very much, but we had gotten off track. With that in mind, Garth then invited me to tour with him throughout 1990 and '91."

"Finally, in 1991 we took a break, a four-day vacation to Maine. It was during this trip that Garth took a picture, which he carries to this day, of me standing on the front porch of a cabin and said, 'I have a picture of the first day you were pregnant.'" He was right. Taylor Mayne Pearl Brooks arrived July 8, 1992, but not without complications.

Sandy wasn't entirely ready to have a baby, she thought. Then something happened at Los Angeles International Airport that jolted her into the awareness of maternal love. She and Garth had just landed at the airport en route to the American Music Awards. She was in her sixteenth week of pregnancy.

And in the busy airport lobby she began to hemorrhage. Garth physically carried her from the baggage claim area, back inside the airport proper, to the ladies' room. The paparazzi were everywhere, anticipating the influx of celebrities for the show. Some even had Garth and Sandy's flight schedule.

Sandy was placed on a little bench that remains in the airport. To this day, she thinks of her ordeal each time she passes it. Her feet were propped up, but the bleeding continued. Sandy realized that she might lose her first baby.

"And I remember lying on that bench and saying, 'Okay, God, when I first found out I was pregnant I didn't want to be. I wasn't ready to take on the responsibility of parenthood. But don't take this baby from me.'

"The ambulance comes, they stretch me on this gurney, and here we go out the back of the airport, and it's all flashes." The freelance photographers had found her. They put their lenses into her face as she lay fighting for her and her baby's lives on the blood-stained cot.

Pam Lewis, Garth's former comanager, tried to

push them away, to make a way for Garth and Sandy. Their desperation showed. That too was photographed.

Sandy wanted to be taken to Los Angeles's famous Cedars Sinai Hospital, but was told it wasn't possible. She instead was taken to a hospital in a high-crime neighborhood. Garth waited for her pacing inside a room with graffiti on the walls and knife slits in the seats. She lay there for forty-five minutes without treatment. Her bleeding had slowed, but continued nonetheless.

In his efforts to take care of Sandy, Garth was unable to appear on the nationally televised awards program. Garth tried to charter a private bus to transport Sandy back to Tennessee. A doctor had told her she would have to rest for eight weeks, and she had no intention of doing that in California. The bus dealer wouldn't release the vehicle because the previous lessee owed $450 for its use. Garth paid the $450 plus his own rental fee. He paid to have Sandy's mother flown from Oklahoma for the long ride to Tennessee.

The bus had a bed in the back, and Garth knelt beside it many times to pray with, and for, his wife and their unborn child. Garth had sent for his regular bus driver, and when that man grew weary, Garth took over the wheel.

And they pressed on. Three days later, mentally and physically spent, Sandy arrived, still on a bus in a bed—with her child still inside her—alive.

And the most vivid reminder of her trauma came

with the delivery of a tabloid magazine. On its cover lay a bleeding, faint, and horizontal Sandy Brooks inside Los Angeles International Airport, helpless on a gurney.

Garth and Sandy found that the relentless hounding of the paparazzi at the airport was to be only the beginning. For the first six weeks of Taylor's life, photographers were trying anything—flying over in helicopters, scaling the fence that surrounded their estate, following their family members, anything and everything—just to get a picture of the newborn. They even followed Taylor on her first outing to Minnie Pearl's house, where Ms. Pearl was introduced to her new namesake. Finally, after six weeks of this, Garth and Sandy decided to release a photo of young Taylor to the *Nashville Banner.*

Garth and Sandy took the following year off from touring to catch their breath, to regroup, and to spend time with precious Taylor. This time of rest soon passed. In September 1993, the Brooks family was getting geared up for the second NBC special, taped at the Texas Stadium.

The televised concert and Garth's production required extra support over the stage and the installation of "Garth bars." Due to structural miscalculations, the infrastructure over the staging collapsed. Sandy remembers how far behind schedule this incident was putting production. "We worked and worked, pulling stuff off the stage. I didn't even take time to eat. The next day I remember feeling sick, thinking it was stress and the work of the previous day. When I was too sick to go to the opening night show, we both realized I was pregnant with our second child.

"It was May 3, 1994; Garth returned home from the European tour just in time for the birth of August Anna Brooks. Her first outing was truly an outing, as she traveled all the way to Australia.

"Our third little girl came as a big surprise." Named Allie Colleen, after Sandy's grandfather and Garth's mother, she was born on July 28, 1996, coincidentally, Sandy's mother's birthday. "We stayed home for the first six weeks of Allie's life and then it was back on the road.

"We felt it necessary to get a 'girl bus.'" Today, Garth and Sandy travel with their three girls, a home-school teacher, and a nanny. "Having the teacher and nanny with us allows the kids to travel with their dad and still get an education . . . and I have the option to go to a show. Both Garth and I feel it's important to be together and close, so we travel with him 95 percent of the time. If Garth's on the road, we're with him. The kids don't know any other way. They grew up with this. They enjoy traveling and seeing different zoos, children's museums, etc. It's a big learning experience for them."

• • •

Sandy and Garth are very firm in their convictions. "We try to support our community," explains Sandy. "There are many things we feel strongly about."

Sandy said that no one in Nashville has stood up for songwriters more than Garth has. And she was behind him when he addressed various lawmaking bodies calling for stricter prosecution of copyright infringement. He was against the sale of recycled recordings, contending that the practice deprived songwriters of second-sale royalties.

"I think I'm as proud of him for that as anything," she said. "The songwriters have their best friend in Garth Brooks."

By 1993, Garth, during a Barbara Walters special, would be criticized for telling the world he had more money than his grandkids' grandkids could ever spend. He didn't make the statement to brag, but to make the point that he remained in the music business solely for the love of the music.

Many years ago, the Nashville press picked up a story about a stranded motorist who was befriended by a stranger who stayed with her until help arrived, then paid for the repair of her car. The motorist later learned the Good Samaritan was Garth.

Sandy's newest project is the Nashville Zoo. As a board member, Sandy has devoted her time to a cause she strongly believes in: children. Neither she nor Garth disclose to the public the amount of money they give to charities. They do it because they believe in the various charities, not to sell more albums.

• • •

On October 26, 1996, Garth and Sandy Brooks stood in front of their family and friends at the Good Shepherd United Methodist Church. They renewed their marriage vows of ten years earlier. The congregation has moved from the building Sandy once cleaned by hand. It's now in a bigger and stronger place—like the love of the couple who said "I do."

"I'm known around the world as being Garth's wife and I'm very proud to be Garth's wife. But all I've ever really wanted to be is a good mother, and I hope in twenty years I can look back and say, 'Yes, I was a good mother.'"

5

Mrs. Glen (Kim) Campbell is a Nashville wife in that her husband's music publishing and recording interests are there; and he is known primarily as a country artist despite his many hits in contemporary Christian and adult contemporary music. I know many Nashville wives who are spiritual, but few who are religious. Kim Campbell is both. She's grounded, and can thoroughly explain how and why she believes as she does.

"I know I'm academic," she said in 1997. "I really want to know the [biblical] Greek, I want to know the Hebrew, I want to know the historical context."

She has a strong passion for faith, and conducts a home ministry. Here we will focus mainly on her role as the wife of one of the best-known entertainers ever to spring from the ranks of country musicians.

In 1980, Kim Campbell (then Kimberly Woolen) was a dancer in Radio City Music Hall's Broadway production of *Snow White and the Seven Dwarfs*. An understudy to one of the supporting actresses, she was never called to go on stage. Instead, she sat quietly each night in full costume in the dark and silent wings. The waiting, as well as the name of the actress Kim waited to replace, is foggy history. Eighteen years later, she can't remember the woman's name.

Kim's time in New York wasn't spent simply *waiting* for opportunity. She spent most of her days *preparing* for it. She rehearsed eight to twelve hours a day, a grueling schedule that eventually resulted in broken blood vessels in her legs.

She also danced at Radio City Music Hall when she wasn't an understudy. "It was generally two shows a day," she recalled. "And during the mornings I would take a ballet class, and then I would go do a show, and then in between shows I would go take a jazz class and then come back that night to do another show."

She was no stranger to discipline. As a child, she had been a straight-A student. She had attained the highest grade-point average in the history of her high school. She could have been a scientist or a scholar. But she majored in dance.

"Yeah, go figure," she said. "I didn't want to get fat." She laughed.

"That's why you majored in dance?"

"Well, I had this dance teacher when I was in high school," she said. "It was rinky-dink dance and she got her degree from East Carolina University and she drove a Corvette. So I thought, she's so thin and beautiful and she drives a Corvette. I want to do that. Is that stupid or what? But that's what a young person would think."

In her early twenties, Kim lived in New York and, like most of her neighbors, walked everywhere she went. She lived briefly on unemployment, ate a lot of peanut butter, and had three roommates. But, unlike most people in Manhattan, Kim managed to save $10,000 during her first year in the Big Apple.

"I would dance all day, and I'd eat like a quart of chocolate chip Häagen-Dazs ice cream and only weighed one hundred pounds," she said. "Those were the good old days."

Not really.

Kim wanted to be out of the grind more than she wanted to be in the spotlight. And so she did what she had done since childhood—she prayed.

"I had always had a relationship with God," she said, "but I don't think that the church as a whole that I was going to [as a child] prepared kids for the evil tricks of the devil. Back then, [church leaders] kind of assumed that you knew what you were supposed to do and what you were not supposed to do. They just didn't talk about it."

Years later, while walking the streets of New York City, Kim prayed for a husband who would take her away. In front of her roommates, amid the crush and clamor that is New York, she spoke out loud and precisely about what she wanted heaven to deliver to her in Gotham.

"I was very specific," she said. "Lord, deliver me from this. Send me a Christian millionaire that I can be in love with and he can be in love with me."

"I had one Jewish girlfriend and one Catholic

girlfriend with me," Kim remembered. "They both looked at me and said, 'I can't believe you prayed like that.'"

Two weeks later she met Glen Campbell.

Ten years earlier, he had been a prime-time network television star with his own variety show. He had subsequently maintained one of the most successful recording and performing careers in the history of contemporary music.

Kimberly Woolen was fixed up with a blind date by Carl Jackson's girlfriend, Lynn Wilford. Carl played in Glen's band.

Glen and his parents were staying at the Waldorf-Astoria Hotel, where Kim, along with Carl and Lynn, went to meet him. Intending to be funny, he burst into the room singing "Like a Rhinestone Cowboy," the lyrics to his biggest hit song. A year later they were man and wife.

"We dated a year, if you want to call that dating," she said. "Today I would call it shacking up or cohabiting, which I do not approve of at all."

They have subsequently enjoyed a happy union that has produced three children and a unified walk in mutual religious beliefs.

"When the kids were little, we just enjoyed Arizona, you know?" she said. "The sun would start to set and we'd say, 'The sun is setting, get in the car.' Then we would drive to the top of the mountain and watch the sun set."

The Campbells spent the majority of their married life as stalwarts of the largest Baptist church in

Phoenix, Arizona. Today they are celebrating Messianic Judaism, a combination of the Jewish faith and a belief in Jesus Christ as the Messiah.

But the courtship and marriage weren't always so joyful.

"Boy, you didn't tell me she was going to be so pretty," were the first words Kim ever heard Glen speak.

He himself was trim and tan and carried a solid physique that belied his forty-five years, three previous marriages, and a whiskey- and drug-soaked, highly publicized affair with Tanya Tucker. Glen and Tanya were on the cover of *People* magazine twice in eleven months.

Kim knew nothing about it.

She was not interested in sensational journalism and never read tabloid publications. She actually did not know much about Glen Campbell except that he was famous to other folks. She could have counted the number of his hit records she knew on one hand with fingers left to spare.

She and Glen, Carl and Lynn, and Glen's parents went downstairs to dine in the elegant Waldorf restaurant, Peacock Alley. She didn't much like how much he drank, but was highly impressed when he said grace before he ate.

"Are you a Christian?" she asked.

"Yes," he said.

"I am, too."

Kim would soon decide that Glen was a carnal Christian, someone willing to partake of the blessings of Jesus Christ without adhering to His standards of behavior. She said that she too, at the time, was a carnal Christian.

Glen, Kim, and the others went to a James Taylor concert and wound up backstage. There she met Taylor's mother and discovered she was from North Carolina, Kim's home state. Kim was making small talk when out of the blue, without provocation, Glen kissed her—right on the mouth—right in the middle of the backstage bedlam.

Their first date was picking up. The acceleration was short-lived.

Glen kept drinking. And drinking. Later, when the couple boarded the elevator at the Waldorf, Glen got off on the wrong floor with people he didn't know. He went with the strangers to their room.

Kim was left with Carl, Lynn, and Glen's parents—most of whom she'd just met.

The group persuaded Glen to leave the strangers' room and return to his own. He continued to drink.

And then he made his romantic gesture.

He told Kim he wanted to jump her bones. Straight out of a Gothic love story, eh?

Glen was already horizontal, on a couch, where he nearly passed out, Kim recalled. She declined his offer about bones and said she was going home. She asked him for taxi fare, and he gave it to her, along with an ultimatum. If she walked out, he threatened, she would never hear from him again.

She left. Her phone was ringing from Glen's call as she entered her apartment. The next day, he invited her to accompany him to his show in Philadelphia.

Kim had lied to her dance captain at Radio City Music Hall in order to accept the blind date with Glen. She lied a second time in order to go to Pennsylvania. A paparazzo spotted Glen and snapped his photograph, and it appeared on the front page of the *New York Post* the next day. Above it ran a headline identifying Kim as a "mystery beauty." When her dance captain saw the picture, Kim was almost fired.

On that Philadelphia date, their second, Glen and Kim slept together for the first time. She said there was no sex.

Days later, when Glen had a few days off from touring, he came to visit Kim again in New York. She was still living in her world of pinched pennies and tuna fish sandwiches. Glen was sending for her in limousines and treating her to caviar. She was the star in an unfolding fairy tale.

Overwhelmed, Kim decided to relent, and began having sex with Glen. She subsequently didn't hear from him for three months. She wondered if she had given herself to a man who had wanted nothing more than her body. She at times felt totally alone in the most densely populated city in the nation. It was a painful learning experience.

At twenty-two, she had been a born-again Christian most of her life. But again she decided she was partaking of biblical blessings while not living by its rules. She was, she surmised again, a carnal Christian. The woman who had casually prayed publicly now prayed a secret prayer for forgiveness.

"God," she said, in contributing to Glen's autobiography, *Rhinestone Cowboy* (Villard Books, 1994), "I thought you sent him, and now I don't know if I'll ever see him again. But you know what's best for me, and if I never see him again, that's probably for my best interest, so I'm going to entrust the whole thing to you."

Glen called the next day to ask her to join him in Lake Tahoe.

Kim was not overly anxious to accept because she had learned about Glen's on-again, off-again stormy relationship with Tanya. During the time Kim had not seen Glen, he and Tanya had made national news after tearing up a hotel room in Louisiana and being threatened with eviction and arrest.

Kim's parents had read the stories. Kim had trouble convincing them that Glen Campbell was a nice guy.

When Kim at last decided to go to Lake Tahoe, she saw firsthand the sea of alcohol in which Glen was sinking. He was a megastar, and everybody wanted to give him a drink. She had always been indifferent to booze, but she decided she would become a teetotaler to help Glen. She hasn't had a drink since 1981. Glen, on the other hand, was smoking marijuana, using cocaine, and really swilling the alcohol.

She spent the rest of the year riding his mood changes. A week before Christmas, Glen asked her to marry him. She accepted, convinced that the God who had made changes in her behavior could do the same for Glen. Ten months later they had a wedding at the twenty-thousand-member North Phoenix Baptist Church.

That too was not without a hitch.

Without consulting Glen, Kim decided there would be no alcohol at their wedding reception. Two days before the ceremony, a furious Glen simply left town. Vanished. His parents, many of his relatives, and Kim's family were in Phoenix for the wedding. Glen was missing in action. The clock was ticking toward the time of the nuptials. Still no sign or word.

He returned to Phoenix hours before the wedding, contacted a friend who owned a restaurant, and persuaded the guy to cater booze to the reception. Glen got drunk and married, in that order, and all of his friends got drunk too. Kim's southern, conservative mother was a bit shaken by Glen's behavior, but not as much as she was by his surprise announcement.

He told her that her daughter was three months pregnant.

The Kim-Glen household was set up. Kim cooked and prayed, and Glen drank. She didn't always know where he was, and she didn't know where his thoughts were when he was with her.

One evening, as she prepared dinner, Glen's chair remained empty. She called the Men's Club at the Phoenix Country Club, learned that Glen was there, and was put on hold for fifteen minutes. Fifteen minutes are an eternity when a young bride has dinner on the stove, a baby in her arms, and a silent telephone held to her ear.

Kim loaded the baby into the car and drove to the men-only resort. She marched with determination into the room, where Glen sat, cigar in mouth and cards in hand. She thrust their newborn child into his arms and fled to the restroom to weep. She suspects she is one of the first women to penetrate that all-male bastion, and certainly the first to bring her child.

Glen had promised he would quit cocaine, and he did—when he was in her presence. But he sometimes sneaked away and returned high. Kim thanks God for the wisdom He gave her in that she refused to talk to Glen about drug abuse while he was using drugs. She waited until he was straight.

Yet Glen was confused. When he became high on the drug, his memory raced to his childhood indoctrination in a country church in his native Billstown, Arkansas. Under the influence of cocaine, he would preach to Kim about her sinful ways, and about his. Kim hated the hypocrisy.

Once, when Kim reprimanded Glen about his drinking, he went into the kitchen and turned a bottle of vodka straight up, guzzling until the bottle fell from his hand and shattered on the floor. She got on her hands and knees and mopped and cried.

In her heart, she knew God could change this man with whom, she was convinced, she was supposed to live. She had prayed for a man, and God had sent Glen. She was determined to see Glen healed from the demons that spawned his reckless ways.

Eventually, Kim sought the power of united prayer among the preachers and parishioners at her church, but that didn't work right away either.

She had long felt that Glen had two personalities: He was a gentleman when sober, a devil when drunk. One refused to acknowledge the other. So she decided she would tape-record the bad to play for the good.

"This is what you said last night," she told him each time.

She turned on a tape recording of his incoherent babble and left the room while he listened to what he didn't want to hear.

But he continued to drink.

He once got out of bed drunk to urinate off a hotel balcony. He locked himself outside in the nude. But Kim stayed and prayed.

Another time Kim found Glen passed out in the bathtub. She was afraid he might drown. But Kim stayed and prayed.

When drunk, he would often think he was sick from something other than alcohol.

"Every time he got sick, he would call some doctor, any doctor, and get penicillin," she said, smiling. Once when he and Kim were in Australia, a doctor came to the hotel room, gave him penicillin and a bottle of blue stuff, and left. Glen took the cap off the blue stuff, chugged it down, and handed it to Kim.

"What do the directions say?" he asked.

"Gargle three times a day," she answered.

Kim stayed and prayed.

Once Glen went on a dry spell, and Kim thought he had been healed of his drinking. Then he came home in a drunken rage.

She claimed the promises of divine healing by clutching a Bible to her breast and verbally rebuking Glen's drunken ways, but he attacked her with words.

Kim hid under the dining room table and draped herself in the tablecloth. Because she couldn't see him, it was easier to ignore him. But not much. He screamed at her through the linen, her only shield.

Kim and Glen were baptized together. They could have gone to a church, but instead they went to an icy river near Glen's childhood home in Arkansas. After immersion in the murky water, they shivered in the used truck owned by Glen's brother, a lay minister.

There had been plenty of fun and fulfilling times, but the alcohol was left over from the life Glen couldn't quite leave.

Then Kim's prayers were answered. Glen decided to sober up.

It happened in August 1986, when Glen was playing a show in Hawaii with the Royal Philharmonic Orchestra. He awakened on yet another day with yet another hangover. Why was this time different?

Kim intends to ask God when she meets Him in heaven.

Glen has been drug and alcohol free ever since.

In retrospect, Kim realizes that there were times during Glen's crazy days when she felt inadequate as a wife—when she blamed herself. She even wondered if she was an inferior Christian. Why, she wondered, was God taking so long to answer her prayers?

She doesn't question God these days as much

as she appreciates Him. She knows He had His own timetable.

She has recently studied biblical interpretations at the Phoenix Seminary. She has overseen home Bible study for fifteen women for three years.

"Messianic Judaism is true biblical Judaism," she said. She'll talk, if questioned, about her past with Glen. But she needs no prodding to talk about her religious faith.

"In the first century, Christianity was a sect called 'The Way,' a form of Judaism. You can read that in the Book of Acts. So our roots really go back to the first-century faith of practice. Romans XI talks about the two olive trees, one cultivated by God, which is the cultivated olive tree of Israel. And there is a wild olive tree, which is the Gentiles, the unbelievers. . . ."

She can go on indefinitely. It isn't my intention to relay Kim's convictions, only their intensity.

Yet her conversion from traditional Christianity, as taught by the Baptist church, to Messianic Judaism was news within church circles. She and Glen had high profiles because they espoused their fundamental born-again message on national Christian television, including programs on the Trinity Broadcast Network and other evangelical forums.

"When you see people who you used to know in the Baptist church, how do they feel about your change?" Tom asked at my request.

"Overall, we've had a very positive response to the things that we're learning and embracing," she replied. "And then there have been a few people who don't understand it, and they like the box that they're in, and don't want to step outside of that. Anybody outside, they're not going to have anything to do with."

"Are they judgmental and legalistic?"

"Yeah, but I understand," Kim said. "I can be pretty sympathetic and understand where people are coming from because they've been taught that. So after a while, you just keep loving people, and they get over it."

"Do you see yourself ever returning to the Baptist church?"

"I don't see myself as separate," she said. "I am definitely part of the body of Christ. I don't see myself as separate, it's more of how do I want to worship and what do I want to practice."

Kim said she learned about Messianic Judaism through personal study of biblical scholars.

"I think there's a great arrogance within our seminaries today," she said. "When I took this course in Hebraic, they gave me a lot of books that I could put in my library. I'd have an *Encyclopaedia Britannica* but not an *Encyclopaedia Judaica,* which is full of text about the first-century Jewish temple practices."

Kim was reared in a Methodist household and participated in Christmas services, but today she doesn't allow Christmas trees or Easter baskets inside her home. She says the Bible teaches against it.

She says her children have handled the changes just fine.

She talks about her children as readily as her

faith. She's a mobile mom who gets up before the household and eventually drives each child to school. She has frequently gone to one event for each of her three children in one day.

"And I love it," she said. "It's the way Glen and I live today."

The woman who can explain basic chemistry or Messianic Judaism can't explain her son's football. But she goes to every game. The woman who majored in dance because someone owned a Corvette drives a Suburban. She drives it everywhere she goes, just like she once walked in New York City.

"My life has changed a lot, hasn't it?" she said, with closure. "My life has changed a lot."

6

My introduction to Tish Cyrus came over the telephone. She called in 1996 wanting a recommendation for a preschool for her four-year-old. She was concerned that her daughter get used to playing with other children, as there are only older siblings on the estate she shares with her husband, Billy Ray Cyrus. I sent my daughter, Adina, to initiate Tish and her daughter into the preschool attended by my grandson. Tish, Billy Ray, and their children came to my grandson's birthday party in April 1997, the star attraction of which was Barney. All of us, excluding Barney, have been friends ever since.

There were 23,622 people living in Ashland, Kentucky, in 1990, the year of the last census. Two years later, on April 3, one of them sat alone, weeping softly over one man on a flickering television screen, the only illumination in her otherwise darkened and tiny bedroom.

Tish could touch the screen, but she couldn't touch him, and neither could the untold millions of other viewers who shared her fascination.

His song and movements, though, were touching most everyone watching. In less than twelve hours, the first television sighting of Billy Ray Cyrus would be the blockbuster buzz of Nashville's Music Row, that three-square-mile conglomeration of record companies, music publishing houses, talent management firms, as well as homes to a regiment of country music stars, has-beens, and hopefuls.

No one in the history of country music has ever enjoyed a more dynamic television debut than Billy Ray Cyrus. He went on to sell three million albums in three months. On January 3, 1993, it was announced that Billy Ray's *Some Gave All* album had been the biggest-selling title by any singer in any musical category in 1992, a feat scored within eight months.

Five days later, on Elvis Presley's birthday, Billy Ray was nominated for five Grammy Awards. The nominations would mark his first major comparison to Elvis, the gyrating genius who sired rock 'n' roll.

Billy Ray's video for his biggest hit, "Achy Breaky Heart," became the most watched in country music history.

The solitary girl in her nondescript bedroom couldn't have predicted those statistics then. And she doesn't care now. That was her man on the screen. He had vowed that he loved her. She had vowed her love for him. He had been with her. And tonight, all she wanted was to be in his presence, to participate in person in the premiere. But Billy Ray, acting on the orders of his management, had left Tish alone, a small-town girl who had two children, no husband, and a nonstop conviction that her heartstrings were being knotted by cable television.

That night, Tish's children sat with their grandmother in an adjacent room, on the other side of a locked door. Tish wanted to see no one except that man on the screen, separated from her by the cold television glass and the six-hour drive to Nashville.

It wasn't fair.

Tish, after all, had sat night after night inside the dingy Ragtime Club, a firetrap in nearby Huntington, West Virginia, where Billy Ray had been the hottest attraction for ten years. (The club, in fact, would burn to the ground in 1997.) He'd spent many of those years commuting to Nashville in a converted bread truck. He often slept inside the rickety vehicle, then spent days knocking on doors, asking someone, anyone, for a break. One year, he spent forty-two weeks making that monotonous Nashville run, then returned to Huntington to grind out his songs for the fans who watched their hometown hero sing for the money that would subsidize next week's trip to Nashville.

Night after night Tish sat in the club. Night after night she went home with him, and listened as he talked of big dreams. She endured his mood swings. She offered encouragement.

They were, at first, just friends. But she eventually held his hand. She eventually gave him her heart, soul, and body—anything to sustain the man whom she felt had talent, and whom she knew she loved.

The love of a lifetime was formed in a matter of months, and has only gotten stronger and stronger.

On the spring 1992 night, the dream was unfolding, not for the woman who'd been by Billy Ray's side, but for those faceless television viewers who'd never even met him.

"I was thinking, 'Oh my God, you know, I'm going to lose him,'" said Tish, in 1997, who became Mrs. Billy Ray Cyrus a year after the television spectacular. "I felt so unwanted by Nashville."

Billy Ray's advisers had decided his career would fare better if the public thought he had no romantic interest. His management saw him as an unattached sex symbol, and he wanted to be certain the world saw him the same way.

Years later, I had a personal experience with Billy Ray's manager. I asked him if Billy Ray could do a show with George Jones, my husband. Billy Ray's manager said he would get back to me.

Then I heard from a reliable source that he didn't want Billy Ray performing with George because Billy Ray was sexy, and he thought George was not.

George didn't think the isolation that was imposed on Billy Ray was a good idea and kept sending word to him not to take this show business nonsense too seriously. But I'm sure Billy Ray never got the messages. He was shielded. There was no room for Tish in the life and career of Billy Ray. His management had decided. The woman behind the man was suddenly on the outside looking in.

And it got worse.

"I felt very left out, and I had a problem with this whole entire business up until maybe 1994," Tish said, from inside the home she shares with Billy Ray, her two children, and their two children.

"Were your feelings so pronounced that the two of you ever came close to breaking up?" I asked.

"Yeah," she sighed. "There were a lot of times that I just wanted out. This is not the life I wanted because, you know, he—he was not mine."

And so she waited while the world applauded. And sometimes, late at night, Billy Ray would call, and he'd tell her he loved her. But he couldn't tell her where he was, or where he would be the next day. He simply didn't know. His life was too fast, a runaway marathon of buses and backstages, of hotel rooms with Spanish furniture and plastic fixtures and the same stale-smelling carpet.

"And he'd tell me what he was doing and I'd be so happy to hear from him," she said. "Then he'd hang up the phone and I'd just cry, just because I hadn't seen him. Sometimes it would be a month and I felt like he was out there on this whirlwind seeing the world, having a big time, and I was at home in this little town. Yeah, I felt left out."

Marriage eventually made the difference.

In 1993, despite the protestations of his management, the heartthrob of throngs of American women became the husband of one. Not one of the millions of women who wanted to be Mrs. Billy Ray Cyrus was even invited to the wedding.

By then, Billy Ray had moved Tish to his Nashville

home. He married her in a small, private ceremony indoors. The ensuing months brought more hits, more money, more children, and a larger house on five hundred wooded acres—a house that is a replica of The Hermitage, Andrew Jackson's home. A fence keeps fans out, and Tish's dreams inside.

Remodeling has been under way for more than a year, and Tish's conversation today is occasionally drowned out by the pounding of hammers and the ripping of saws. The house had an indoor swimming pool that Tish wanted to be outside. Workmen tore down the pool's glass walls as we visited.

"You can't get a suntan with an indoor pool," she said.

Tish is a beauty queen who could sit atop anybody's throne. At twenty-nine, she looks twenty-one, a buxom, blonde bombshell straight from the pages of *Cosmopolitan* magazine. She's a cover girl whose magnetism leaps off the page, but she's also a warm and loving person whose inner beauty is as striking as her outer. She once considered a career in modeling after her move from Kentucky to Nashville.

Billy Ray said it would give her something to do while he was on the road. But it would have also made for obligations—obligations she didn't want when Billy Ray was in town. So she gave up the modeling, and any other career, to wait for Billy Ray while he was gone, so she could wait on him while he was home.

The two live as one.

She talks incessantly about Billy Ray, like a

lovestruck teenager. He's the only thing she talks about, and lives for—except for the kids.

"But I sometimes see him as one of the kids," she said. "He's such a devoted father, and he just plays with them like he's one of them, all day long. People would have no idea what the real Billy Ray is like.

"I couldn't imagine not being married to him," she said, staring into space. "I couldn't imagine being more happy."

"But what's it like being coupled to a sex symbol?" Tish was asked, and pressed as to whether she thought other women made passes at Billy Ray when she wasn't around.

"They do it when I'm around," she said, "right in front of my face."

But it doesn't bother her. She's secure. She knows she loves her man, and he loves her. Nothing, she said, but nothing, could make her believe he'd ever be unfaithful. If someone showed her a picture of Billy Ray in a compromising situation, Tish would swear it was trick photography. All that trust for a man at whom women throw motel keys and panties while he's onstage.

"Am I naive?" she asked.

"Of course not," I said.

Not even another woman's book about a tryst with Billy Ray has swayed Tish's trust.

My Billy Ray Cyrus Story: Some Gave Too Much, the book by Kari Reeves, never reached Tish. Reeves talks about having slept with Billy Ray while he was married to someone before Tish, and how he left her bed to call his former wife, to whom he pledged his love.

"I didn't read that book," said Tish, "not one sentence. I don't think Billy Ray did either. It doesn't matter. All that happened in the eighties. This is now."

"But what if he really did cheat," I pressed. It was again noted that the man, in 1990s parlance, is a "hunk." A sizzling sex symbol. Can he be expected to be faithful forever? Can't someone make a mistake?

She pondered the question longer than any other.

"Oh my gosh," she suddenly imploded. "I wouldn't be here if he did. I guess I can't say that, because I have never been in that position, but first of all, I can't imagine that happening, and if it did I don't know that I could . . ."

Her speech was rapid and runaway. It was obvious that the mere idea of adultery, the curse of twentieth-century marriages, was totally foreign to Tish Cyrus.

"I think," Tish said, of husbands in general, "if that's the life they want to live, why not just get a divorce? I mean, why not say, 'I want a divorce,' and then go play the field?

"There's no way Billy Ray could do it [be unfaithful]," she snapped. "God, when could he do it? I mean, he calls me thirty times a day from the road."

I'm convinced.

She knows some might think she has her head in

the sand, but she knows her heart's in caring hands. And she knows people don't know her husband, not the way she does.

The two grew up ten miles apart, although they didn't meet until Tish was twenty-two, and went to hear the singer that had eastern Kentucky rocking.

"He was a star even then," she said. "I mean, he didn't even have a record deal, and people wanted his autograph."

Tish doesn't drink, and neither does Billy Ray. From the Kentucky bandstand, he watched her watch him, night after night, for perhaps three months.

Then one night he approached. He told her he had noticed her sobriety inside the rowdy honky-tonk.

He asked if he might ask a personal question.

She said yes.

He asked if he might take her home.

She said yes.

"I'll never forget it because I thought he was a little strange," Tish said, matter-of-factly.

"Why?"

"How many people just walk up to a total stranger and ask, 'Can I ask you a question, can I give you a ride home?'" she said. "But then again, I did say yes."

The two drove to the dwelling Tish shared with her mother and children, and sat outside until almost dawn.

"We just talked," she said. "He told me about this record deal he had in Nashville, and all that he hoped would happen to him."

Despite the upcoming months of separation, Tish would eventually learn that she and Billy Ray were somehow never apart.

Tish grew up involved in virtually every activity offered by her public school—tap dancing, cheerleading, piano lessons, ballet, and more.

Today, she rarely leaves her house when Billy Ray is touring. She almost never leaves when he's at home.

"We joke that we never leave the compound," she said. "And I guess it's the truth. Maybe we go out once a week to eat in Franklin [a Nashville suburb], but that's about it. Billy Ray never goes anywhere except to get a haircut, unless he's touring. We hardly ever even go to Nashville."

Tish leads a charmed life. She gets up around 11:00 A.M. after sleeping upstairs with her two children. She joins them after sitting up late with Billy Ray.

"I'm a late sleeper," she said. "I have to have ten hours or I'm not worth much."

Her nanny removes the youngsters when they awaken, and Tish goes back to sleep. By the time she goes downstairs to start her day, the children and Billy Ray are somewhere on the sprawling grounds.

The father and youngsters ride horses, drive gasoline-operated machinery, hike, gather rocks, pick flowers, ride bicycles, and even do some unimportant things. Tish again called Billy Ray the most devoted father she's ever met.

She has a live-in cook, and sometimes she cooks

too. It doesn't necessarily matter, as Billy Ray and the kids are almost always late for meals.

"He has no sense of timing," she said. "It's one of the things that makes me most mad about him. I might make supper, and he and the kids will come in two hours late to eat.

"You ask me about my life," she went on. "He is my life, him and my kids. And that's all I want. I couldn't be happier."

"Do you help make the decisions?" she was asked.

"Yeah, I do," she said quickly. "Just everything. When he's in the studio doing demos or when he's being pitched songs or whatever . . . I mean, he would never just go record without my input. I mean, we kind of like just solve that together. We'll sit down and listen to all of the tapes and then . . ."

"Do you go to the recording sessions, too?"

"Yes," she said, "I go to a lot of them. I didn't go to the last three, his newest three, and I'll tell you why: He actually did them all in one day."

Tish could not have made it through Billy Ray's premarital absenteeism without the help of her mother, Loretta Finley.

"And I couldn't make it without her now," she said. "I've got to have my mom, and she's got to have me. I was the only child. My mom always lives with me."

And so Mom does—in a house that Billy Ray provided on his property.

Tish has one job outside the home. It's a few hundred yards away, and she drives her pickup to work.

She can commute on a couple of tanks of gasoline a year.

From inside what was once an abandoned schoolhouse, she oversees the operation of the Billy Ray Cyrus Fan Club. She's the president, and even draws a salary, although she doesn't know why. She'd do it for free.

"I think he's one of the most misunderstood people on the planet," she said. "People have no idea how gentle and sensitive and caring he is. He's always being asked to do a benefit show and he always says yes. I've never known a more giving human being. And they don't know all he went through in Kentucky to get here. They think he's just an overnight success."

She hates the public misconception, and blames it on Billy Ray's former management company, who, she said, kept Billy Ray away from the Nashville music establishment. She implied that his old career molders were trying to build an image of aloofness—to create a mystique—perhaps similar to the mystery that surrounded Elvis. And, she freely admits, while Billy Ray is polite, he is not a pushover.

(She and Billy Ray's former manager are on civil terms, and she says she has no ill will against him today.)

I personally have felt sorry for him, and the bad rap he's taken from the press and recording industry just because he wouldn't play politics. I mean, let the man stand on his talent, not his willingness to capitulate. I respect his stand.

I know for a fact that Billy Ray has done almost every charity show that any radio station has asked him to do. Yet he doesn't get radio airplay because he won't schmooze with the radio consultants, those people who advise radio stations what songs to put on their playlists.

And Billy Ray is shy. People mistake that shyness for conceit. I hate that.

And if the press can't get the facts, they'll write their opinions. I think there is a jealousy factor involved, and so does Tish.

But forgive me. This chapter is about Tish.

She told me that she and Billy Ray never quarrel.

"That sounds like a lie but it's not," she said, softly but firmly. "As a matter of fact I've maybe heard him raise his voice hardly ever, which kind of drives me crazy because I'd rather just get into it. He does not. I mean, I'm willing to yell and scream, but he's not . . ."

"He's not confrontational?"

"He's not, and that drives me crazy too," she went on. "He hates confrontations. I mean, he very seldom will do anything on a confrontation. He has never yelled at me. Never."

"Well, hasn't he hurt your feelings?"

"Yes," she finally said, "he's hurt my feelings. I can't remember how."

"Well, is there any stress in this marriage at all?"

"No. I know if I ever do get stressed out about anything he'll go, 'Tish, why are you stressed? We have the most perfect life. You should just be thankful.'"

"Do you think your relationship ever suffers from overexposure? I mean, he's practically your whole life."

"No, I don't think so," she said, without missing a beat.

"A lot of wives have told me they're glad to see their husbands come home, but they're also glad to see them go back on the road," I said.

"Oh no, that's not me. I always dread to see him leave."

Her responses were too rapid, her voice too sensitive, to have been anything but sincere.

I couldn't find any apparent fault with her or her marriage. Hers is among the most simple of lives of all the Nashville wives. She's at peace.

Living back in that woods, separated from everyone except her family, Tish reminded me of a fulfilled pioneer woman with modern conveniences. She knew how to please her man, and that pleased her very much.

And she seemed to focus on the simple things. The day before my arrival, she had planted flowers by the gate just for me. She told me I could pick one as I left. She often works in the garden, and, like the rest of her family, strolls through the natural beauty that is her Eden on earth.

Billy Ray and Tish, I thought, were similar. Each was physically beautiful. People are so consumed with the beauty of their features that they overlook the beauty of their souls.

Tish said she was concerned about the response this chapter about her would bring.

"People won't believe that we're this happy," she said. "But we are. What else can I say? I have to tell the truth, no matter what they think."

7

I first met Janine Dunn in the office of our mutual financial manager during the early 1990s. She was filled with energy and sass, and was complaining about her husband. Her words and attitude reminded me of some of my own comments about Jones. I instantly liked her.

I occasionally run into her around Nashville. With each encounter, we swear we're going to get together for lunch soon, but we probably won't. A lot has happened since we first met, in that she had her first child four years ago, and she has moved her mother, sister, and Ronnie's two children to town. She is still spirited, but much more domesticated. She likes to be at home, with family. I like that, too. Janine is not any less spirited. She just seems to be more focused, like a Martha Stewart with attitude.

The neighborhood is a stone's throw from Williamson County, the richest in Tennessee, and sports groves of trees hiding towering houses, the most modest of which are mansions. (The others are bona fide estates.)

Janine Dunn and husband Ronnie, the vocal

backbone of country music's hottest duo, Brooks & Dunn, are dining tonight inside a turn-of-the-century stable that the Dunns remodeled into a recreational hall. The rustic structure's rafters fill with recorded versions of Janine's twenty favorite songs, recorded earlier by Ronnie to commemorate their anniversary. Outside, a soft rain falls on the sprawling acreage. Inside, Janine's tears flow as she looks at her plate, filled from a menu Ronnie prepared personally. She is overcome with joy. Romance is everywhere.

Marital bliss was not always as pronounced for Janine, whose days of rocky partnership are as foreign to her now as the days of financial stress. Both are ancient history—history Janine has determined will never repeat itself.

The couple, with four-year-old daughter Haley, frequently walk their seventeen-acre woods where they closely watch carpenters and other craftsmen fashion a home into the shape of things to come—better things. These days, though, it's hard for things to get better for Janine and Ronnie.

The most prestigious award within the country music industry, "Entertainer of the Year," is bestowed by the Country Music Association in the fall, the Academy of Country Music in the spring. Brooks & Dunn have won the coveted prize during each of its last three events.

Prosperity has sat well with the couple, who are overseeing the remodeling of their fourth Tennessee home in nine years. But remodeling is a misnomer. The name of this construction is expansion. Workmen raise ceilings, add wings, cut windows the size of those at department stores, and that's only the beginning. The Dunns, guardians of southern modesty, don't talk about their holdings any more than cattlemen talk about the size of their herds. In rural, polite society, it just isn't discussed.

The recreation hall is perhaps 7,500 square feet. Square footage is irrelevant to the main house, with its angular architecture and beam ceilings. Measuring floor space would be as meaningless as recording the dimensions of a metropolitan museum.

When finished, the place will be a palace. The master bedroom closet is bigger than most apartments in midtown Manhattan.

This house is destined for the pages of *Architectural Digest*, and is being built one day at a time—much the way the Dunns built a marriage that has withstood ravages analogous to the Civil War battles that were fought on what is now their front lawn.

"I'm doing this interview for this book," said Janine, "because I want women to know that if our marriage could make it, anybody's can. Nobody had more problems. But love prevailed, and the marriage survived. And it will survive forever."

Success, marital or financial, was late in coming for the Dunns. Pain was the Dunns' former companion as much as prosperity is their present one.

Janine, in consenting to tell her story, insisted that it begin at the beginning.

She remembers it wasn't love at first sight for

Ronnie and her, and for good reason: They can't agree on their first sighting.

Ronnie insists he remembers their first sighting vividly for a very distinctive reason: He didn't like what he saw. He says Janine, who had hired his band and him for a private party, gave him the cold shoulder and a slender paycheck.

"I thought she was a snob," Dunn said.

Janine, years earlier, had been a waitress in Tulsa, Oklahoma, where she was born and reared in middle-class surroundings. She met a customer, coal-mining magnate Bill Patch, in the early 1970s. A four-year marriage ensued, and Bill took his bride to his eleven-bedroom estate in Welch, Oklahoma, a coal-mining community where Bill had somewhat of a monopoly; he owned the only mine.

Bill and Janine lived a fairy-tale life within 17,000 square feet on six hundred acres whose pristine beauty was striped by a mile-long runway for jets carrying festive partygoers on and off the manor. The spread was Oklahoma's answer to television's South Fork.

Bill was amused by Johnny Cash's 1976 recording "One Piece at a Time," a novelty ditty about an autoworker who builds a car by stealing parts from an assembly line one piece at a time. Each part is from a different model year, and Bill decided to hand-build a Cadillac like the one described in the song. The car was intended as a comical eyesore, and Bill donated it to Cash. It sat for years inside the Johnny Cash Museum near Nashville.

Janine was twenty-one years old, the wife of a

multimillionaire, and, because of that silly car, became a friend of one of country music's most time-proven legends.

Then it all began to crumble.

Bill Patch developed cancer. Two and a half years after the diagnosis, Janine was a widow in a giant house from which she oversaw a small empire—and not too successfully.

She gradually lost the coal business because she followed some advice that she suspects was unwise. And since she had lost the business, she eventually lost the house. Her net worth shrank to nothing. And the losses came in the most painful way—gradually.

Janine struggled to juggle money to keep the failing mining operation alive. Watching her fortune slowly deplete, she borrowed to throw good money after bad. In time, she'd be forced to sell her splendid home for a fraction of its worth at auction. Janine wept amid the auctioneer's chant as bidding on the five-million-dollar showplace never got zealously into six figures. Bidders liked the place, but not its remote location. Potential buyers wanted a mansion in the countryside—as long as the countryside wasn't as removed as Welch.

"Bill had told me very little about how to run the coal business, and I wasn't interested anyhow," Janine reflected, analyzing her financial demise. "When you're a woman by yourself who has been thrown into a situation like that, you've got this man's business that you don't like. You don't know anything about it and yet it's your only form of livelihood. Obviously, it's a tough thing, but you try to succeed and it's really bad because you have to trust somebody. My father would say, 'Maybe I could help, maybe I could go and run the mines.' But my dad was retired and I didn't want him to be burdened with that and I—I just didn't know what to do."

Janine even had to sell all her furniture, and most of her personal property, to satisfy creditors.

The stress would eventually bring Ronnie and Janine closer together. A few more years, and a walk on a psychological tightwire, would pass first. By the time they met, Janine would look back on a life in which she'd lived in economic modesty, been married, rich, widowed, and broke. She would be barely thirty.

The story of Ronnie and Janine began with their bonding as friends shortly after one of his shows in Oklahoma (they still can't agree on which show). He had moved there as a young man from Texas.

Ronnie says he remembers how impressed he was with Janine's knowledge of country music, and how she discussed it like a scholar, not a fan.

"Her questions were intelligent. I couldn't get over how much she knew, and how she made me think."

Eventually, she made him think about moving to Nashville in order to advance his career. Persistent, she wouldn't let the thought go away.

Ronnie was separated and on the brink of divorce. He would eventually lose his marriage, but was determined to stay near his children. Consequently, the move to Tennessee, for him, was out of the question.

So Ronnie stayed in Oklahoma, and Janine began to interact more heavily with friends in Nashville, including the Cashes. June Carter Cash, Johnny's wife, introduced Janine to John Schneider, costar of television's *The Dukes of Hazzard*, a hit comedy.

She traveled with Schneider for a short while, visiting a motion picture set for a film starring Schneider and Cash and seeing all of the show business sights. During this period, she might typically be in Las Vegas's bright lights, while her new friend Ronnie was wailing in Oklahoma's darkened honky-tonks. These dumps were once called "knife and gun clubs," but not anymore. Nobody bothers with knives. In those days, Ronnie and Janine were miles, and worlds, apart.

For Janine, there was another dating relationship with an older gentleman. Friends thought that he might be "the one." Whispers circulated that Janine might marry, because, some said, she was weary of being a widow. Janine threw a lavish sixtieth birthday party for the man, and Ronnie was invited to sing. Ronnie didn't show, for reasons he can't recall. The party, and Janine's life, went on without him.

Janine and her companion were frequent visitors to one of Oklahoma's sprawling lakes. Ronnie occasionally saw them en route to the water from inside the retail liquor store where he worked. It was the last day job he would ever hold. The move to Nashville and the eventual founding of Brooks & Dunn were about three years away.

Ronnie and Janine still were not an item, indeed, not even an idea—at least not as far as she was concerned. By 1988, Ronnie had developed a crush on the coal miner's widow, although he had told no one. He learned that she would celebrate the Fourth of July on the lake, so Ronnie, with members of his band, crashed her holiday merriment.

"He was drunk on tequila," she recalled. "I just thought he was the funniest thing I ever saw. Comes up, drunk as a coot in cowboy boots, a T-shirt, a bandana, a cowboy hat and yellow Jams [shorts]."

She still has the Jams.

Ronnie confesses his unexpected arrival had a secret agenda.

"I had that mad crush on her," he insisted. He waited an entire year before telling her.

"I waited because my marriage was about that far from going away," he said, holding two fingers close together. "It was gone, gone, period."

When he thought the time was finally right, Ronnie startled Janine with the news that he was in love. With her. This is how he broke the news:

He and his band had played still another dingy dive, this one in Miami, Oklahoma. Janine and friends went to hear him. After the show, she gave Ronnie a lift to his car.

He told her to pull off the road, that he had something to say. Curious, Janine wheeled into a farmer's driveway that neither can find today. Inside the car, Ronnie declared his feelings.

"I mean, it was completely out of the blue," Janine said. "I didn't even suspect. I was completely dumbfounded."

"How did you react?"

"Well, I didn't want to miss a good story," she said. So she listened while a hoarse singer spoke words that are velvet to every woman's ear.

Years later, she answered an unasked question.

"I never touched him," she said, stressing the propriety of their affection. Ronnie's marriage was dying of itself. Neither she nor he wanted to do anything to hasten the death.

"I told her that night, 'I'm headed for a divorce,'" Ronnie recalled.

"When that happens, call me," Janine said firmly.

She didn't see him again for months. His confession in the farmer's driveway had left her speechless. The two didn't even talk by telephone for weeks.

By the time Janine finally heard from Ronnie, he had moved out of his house. His divorce was imminent. There was still no dating between them.

Janine today rolls with laughter about an incident that preceded Ronnie's announcement of love. She had been inside a Tulsa bookstore owned by a man who fancied himself a psychic. Ironically in an aisle reserved for fiction, the proprietor told Janine, without asking, that she would fall in love with a tall and lanky man.

Janine left the store that day with her mother, and

the two pondered who such a man might be. Minutes passed before Janine could even think of a rangy man among her acquaintances. The only name that finally popped into her mind was Ronnie's.

"It would be a cold day in hell before I'd ever marry him," she said. Her mother matter-of-factly agreed. The two continued shopping.

By early 1990, a divorced Ronnie Dunn and widowed Janine Patch had something other than friendship in common. When Ronnie told her again that he loved her, she replied she loved him too. Romance had been a long time coming, restrained by stop-and-go caution characteristic of two people afraid to try love, and more afraid not to.

Janine had astonished her family by declaring that Ronnie was the one, and subsequently sought the acceptance of her best Nashville friends, the Cashes. Janine approached June with trepidation. The word Janine chooses to describe June's reaction to Ronnie is "spectacular."

"She was spectacularly unimpressed," Janine said. "She said, 'Okay, he can sing, he's a good singer and he might make a couple of hits or whatever but he probably won't be a big star and even if he is, what are you going to do when you are with him climbing up to the top and then he gets there and leaves you for a twenty-two-year-old?'"

It was noted that the same question could have been asked of June when she agreed to marry Johnny Cash almost thirty years earlier.

"That was the point," Janine said. "She was

transferring a lot of what had happened to her to this specific incident and all of her kids have had relationships that were not perfect."

Janine was asked if she got the approval she desperately sought from Cash himself.

"He never said a word," she said.

Dejected, Janine returned with her fiancé to Oklahoma where they lived together.

"It was so depressing to me because I wanted them [the Cashes] to like him so much," she said.

One of the last things the Dunns did before permanently leaving Oklahoma was to marry inside Janine's expansive house, not long before its sale. She derived enough money to satisfy creditors and subsidize a move to Nashville—a move Ronnie still didn't want to make. But the pressure to go was mounting.

Former University of Tulsa teacher Tim DuBois, from nearby Grove, Oklahoma, had heard Ronnie sing in a Tulsa nightclub. About that same time, Tim had become president of Arista Nashville, the southern division of the legendary record label founded by Clive Davis. Tim had recently signed to the label a young country singer named Alan Jackson.

Tim called Ronnie to Grove and told him something he had never told another artist—that Ronnie should move to Nashville at any cost.

Ronnie still refused to leave Oklahoma and his children, and that put stress on the young marriage. The widow of a multimillionaire, now strapped herself, was married to a singer who performed for as little as one hundred dollars a night. She sat many nights inside the firetraps where he played, refusing drunken advances from men who didn't know she was with the man onstage.

Ronnie kept singing, and Janine kept insisting that he move to Nashville. A country singer who won't try it in Nashville is like a film actor who won't try it in Hollywood, she thought. He may be good, but only a small following will ever know. She wanted her husband's talent to be celebrated, not a well-kept secret.

Their recurring dispute over the necessity to relocate became a recurring and sore subject. The new lovers became old hands at fighting.

"If the president of a record label urged me to move to Nashville I'd be packing right now," Janine argued.

"The president of the record label isn't the father of my children," Ronnie retorted.

Reluctantly, Ronnie finally agreed to "check out" Nashville, accepting an invitation to examine an apartment owned by Tim. Ronnie had visited Nashville earlier and left songs with prospective producers, to no avail. He had found out that he couldn't commute his way into major-league country music.

Tim offered to let them live in his place free of charge, but the place was far too small for two adults, two children, and furniture. They spent less than five minutes inside.

"We walked out of Tim's little place and driving away I was so upset and so depressed that I threw my Coke out the car window, not realizing that the window was up," Janine said. "I spilled it all over the car and the kids."

Nearly hysterical, she blotted cola and tears.

The family had enough money to return to Oklahoma, and did.

"I got a call from June Carter one day out of the blue and she says, 'Honey, would you come and live in the log house?'"

The "log house," then owned by the Cashes, was a two-story, 5,000-square-foot answer to a prayer. It was rent-free.

The Dunns now had a roof over their heads, but still no money in their pockets. Then Ronnie got a songwriting deal at Sony Tree, and was paid an advance against royalties of $250 a week.

They ate a lot of spaghetti.

Economics had forced Ronnie to leave his children in Oklahoma. He couldn't put a price on how much he missed them. During the Dunns' first year in Nashville, they put 100,000 miles on their car driving back and forth to see his two kids, both of whom were in grade school. He usually drove while Janine read to him aloud, and the books were usually about music or musicians.

"And as I look back, those rides and that simple reading to him was the most romantic time of all," she said.

There were several false starts for Ronnie. Record executives made appointments and promises that they didn't keep. He went through Nashville's grist mill of frustration. Overcome, he once put his foot through a car windshield, and once smashed borrowed drinking glasses. Janine cleaned up the pieces.

The union of Brooks & Dunn, consummated by Tim DuBois, is now old news. Tim liked Kix Brooks's animation, and Ronnie's singing. The first album, *Brand New Man*, and its namesake single record shot to number one. The duo was an instant success. It was impossible to tune to a country music station without hearing Ronnie's wailing tenor. A short six years later, Brooks & Dunn would become the third-biggest-selling duo in the history of all recorded music.

Ronnie had worked a lifetime for the success. Janine had struggled throughout their two-year marriage waiting for the miraculous break. Then both saw the other side of victory. A dark side. Neither Ronnie nor Janine had ever planned Ronnie's becoming part of a duo.

Janine had thought that if Ronnie made the big time, she would travel with him, and might even be his manager. Suddenly, she felt as if she'd been airbrushed out of the picture she'd helped to paint. They had spent hours on those Nashville-Oklahoma trips, talking and fantasizing about the glory to come. And now she was out, Kix was in, and Janine was left alone in the log cabin.

"I was very traumatized," she said. "It was more the way . . . his manner of announcing it, and it was more the attitude changes that I had seen coming out of him since the duo thing started. I mean, I was a newlywed and all of a sudden not only is he a duo, he's a duo with someone we don't even know. We're in a strange town, away from my family, his family, and his way of putting it to me was, 'You ain't gonna be on that bus.' That's how he put it, and that's what tore my heart in two. I felt extremely betrayed."

Then there was the videotaped production of the song.

"Brand New Man," Janine believed, was written about Ronnie and her, as its theme is about a man who is transformed by the power of love. Janine assumed she would be in the video.

Ronnie never gave her participation a thought, and instead had his own ideas about the production involving a glamorous girl wearing ribbons and a white dress. That also left Janine blue.

"You jerk," I thought, "you don't want me in the video. If you don't want me in the video, you can at least pick a story that depicts some great love story like ours."

The Dunns had been together for two years. Janine felt totally betrayed in a matter of weeks. Today, she suspects that she could have been mistaken about some things, but there was no mistaking the pain, then or now.

"I wasn't mature enough to handle some things," she said.

"And you felt success had changed him?" she was asked.

"Absolutely," she snapped. "He was wild, he was

arrogant, he was mean, he was coldhearted, he was really an asshole."

Janine insists she literally wanted to die in 1990. Her husband was on radio, television, the concert trail, at the top of popularity surveys. He was everywhere except at home. She lived for telephone calls from Ronnie on the road.

"And you know," she said, "he would call me and say, 'I'm having a great time, oh my God, we're doing this and we're doing that and God this is just great.' And all I wanted to hear him say was, 'I miss you so much.' I didn't want him to call and say how much fun he was having with the boys and how drunk he had gotten last night and how many strip bars they went to. Gosh, that's really reassuring for any wife, especially a new wife. It was a very difficult time and I certainly didn't have the maturity to handle it."

Ronnie insists that Janine was missing his message, that his nightly calls always stressed how much he loved her. There was mutual counseling, and Janine's repeated readings of *Men Are from Mars, Women Are from Venus*. And more counseling.

Janine thought she hated Ronnie, and told him so, the first time they went to a counselor whom they largely credit with saving their marriage. She didn't even want to hear Ronnie's side. But she did, and learned that Ronnie's dad was an alcoholic and about the theory of ACOAA—Adult Children of Alcoholics Anonymous.

"It was all brand new to me," she said, regarding

the ACOAA theory and how it pertained to Ronnie. "I knew nothing at all about that, and it really turned on some lights for me."

The counselor said that on an "anger scale" most folks walk around at a "one or two," and don't blow up until they reach "nine or ten." The adult child of an alcoholic walks around at a "six," and consequently gets angry easier than adult children of non-alcoholics.

There is no point in continuing to itemize the conflicts of the young Mr. and Mrs. Dunn. The more his career succeeded, the more their marriage flirted with failure. Very soon, divorce was discussed about as frequently as dinner plans.

When asked how often she thought about leaving, Janine was clear.

"Every day," she said. "Just every day."

She claims that Ronnie had, and still has to a lesser degree, a problem conveying his feelings.

"Not passion," she said. "He's very passionate. We've always had a great sex life. But he doesn't know how to be emotional."

She points to the time when their troubles were essentially behind them and he gave her an eight-carat diamond ring. There was no ceremony. They weren't even alone. In a crowded and very public place he said, "Here," and flipped her a box.

"And then, when I least expect it, he can be so sweet," she continued.

"What's the sweetest recollection you have?" I asked through Tom.

She thought.

"One time, when he got an award, I've forgotten which one, but he was on national television, and in his acceptance speech he looked at me in the audience, and he thanked me, and he said, 'This one is for you.'"

Five words spoken before 20 million people and Janine melted.

Ronnie's daughter, Whitney, unhappy in Oklahoma, came to live in the Dunns' unhappy home in 1992. Her presence, in those days, was one more brick in the wall of a crumbling marriage. (Ronnie's son, J.W., stayed with his mother in Tulsa.)

Janine had never reared a child. She suddenly had a thirteen-year-old stepdaughter. The females fought, Dunn went back on the road, and all wondered how the trinity could go on.

And then Janine got pregnant.

At thirty-eight, after years of thinking she was infertile, Janine conceived. She didn't know whether to call for an appointment with a nanny, psychologist, divorce lawyer, or hit man.

Haley Dunn's birth made an immeasurable difference in the lives of Janine and Ronnie. The counselors and psychologists had applied academic training to the Dunns' marriage. The real savior had no credentials other than insomnia and dirty diapers.

"Haley saved our marriage," Janine said. "She made the difference."

It was that sudden. It was that final.

Ronnie and Janine had never shared the story of

their troubled past until now. Visiting their home today, it's hard to imagine that friction, much less conflict, much less outright war, ever existed.

Ronnie is on the road less these days and in his living room more. He and Kix have reduced their touring schedules to be with family. Repeated visits with the Dunns have never revealed a raised voice.

There are family dinners, overseeing Whitney's homework, teaching Haley to talk, discussion of dental braces, arguing with the plumber, and all the rest that comprise that wonderfully chaotic blend of household and home.

Inside, four people will not live separately together—but together as one. The Dunns use the same honesty in describing their new lives as they use in lamenting their old.

Simply put, there was a time—too long a time—when it seemed it just couldn't work. Circumstances have changed because Ronnie and Janine have changed.

"I love him more than he knows," she said, "just as he is more talented than he knows. And I can't imagine this family not being together. I mean, that's pretty simple, but that's how it is. Things are now as good as they once were bad, so I think you get the idea. And yes, I'd have to say that it began with the birth of Haley. I never, I mean never, thought about having a child. Now, we're occasionally thinking about adopting another.

"Life is good now and there isn't much else to tell, except that it's good and getting better."

8

I have not personally met Mrs. Jeff (Gregg) Foxworthy. I used to watch her husband's network television show, and I admired how he never lost his humble demeanor, even while doing his act. As they say in the South, he never got above the "roots of his raisin'."

Jeff played Nashville on New Year's Eve 1997. I asked a mutual friend to ask Gregg if she would be in my book.

Tom Carter and I were set to meet her in her home in Atlanta in February 1998, but George fell sick. I eventually had to take George to our Florida home where he could bask in a warmer climate to shake his respiratory problems.

So Tom met Mrs. Foxworthy without me. He tape-recorded their conversation, then brought the tapes to me so that I could cowrite the story.

Even Gregg's speaking voice percolates. I've read where joy is the eternal sign of the presence of God. If that's true, this woman indisputably knows the God about whom she talks so freely. Her electric personality leapt off the audiotape. I could "hear" her every smile as I listened to her recorded voice. Tom told me I was often right, and that he had remembered many of her recurring and joyful grins.

Jeff and Gregg, like Glen and Kim Campbell, are devoutly religious as well as spiritual.

They preach what they believe by living it. Lives as happy as theirs have to have a special relationship with the eternal someone special.

People are praying inside a sprawling building with a beam roof in a lavish Atlanta neighborhood. The building is not a church, and the people are not a congregation. The setting is the home of Mr. and Mrs. Jeff Foxworthy and their seven- and four-year-old daughters. In a matter of minutes, breakfast will be consumed, and Jeff will drive the youngsters to school. Before he does, he'll help dress each, and attend to all of the little-girl necessities except for the tying of bows. Despite his wealth of creative talent, his attempts at feminine bows resemble a bulky knot tied by an aged sailor with arthritis.

But none of the activity described above will happen until the family reads the Bible and prays. That's the usual beginning of each day in a household unusually rooted in faith. The Foxworthys believe the adage "the family who prays together stays together."

Morality and spirituality like theirs is a rarity in show business, and even in contemporary American life.

Jeff and Gregg have been married for thirteen years. They've been together for fifteen. Jeff is one of the world's foremost stand-up comedians. Reaching the pinnacle of his craft was marked by the landing of his own prime-time network television show. It aired on both NBC and ABC. A stand-up comic getting his own network situation comedy slot is like an actor starring in a Steven Spielberg movie. It doesn't get any better.

Gregg is an actress, and the couple has gone through the show business mill. He worked the dingy and smoke-filled comedy clubs where the biggest laugh was the idea that he might get paid. She did minor movies, local plays, and commercials. But their marriage never suffered the pitfalls that go with climbing the show business ranks. They are, and have always been, drug and alcohol free. Infidelity has never even been a consideration, Gregg insists.

"I've never doubted him for a moment, and I know that sounds unbelievable," she said. "He's a man of God. He was raised Christian. We're Protestant Christian and that's a very important aspect of our lives.

"Besides the Bible study every morning, we have couples Bible study," she added. "He's also in a men's Bible study group. Our children go to Christian school. It's a very important part of our life."

She mentioned the social time she and her family spend with Christian members of the Atlanta Braves baseball team. She said she's aware of many successful marriages, and each has a common thread: God is at its center.

When Jeff's career was in its infancy, he would leave tiny comedy clubs immediately after his act to walk in the middle of the night to a modest motel. He refused to stay after his act for even a soft drink nightcap, Gregg insisted.

"He would tell me that he was away from home and he was lonely," Gregg said. "And he'd tell me he realized that the situation could make him vulnerable, so he wouldn't even allow himself to be tempted. The thought of Jeff's being unfaithful doesn't even cross my mind. I trust him completely."

She has a schoolgirl's enthusiasm when discussing Jeff and her children. She admits that she sometimes gets the chronology wrong. But that doesn't matter. She knows how things turned out, and she's overwhelmed.

Their marriage may be rock solid, but that doesn't mean it hasn't been rocky. They have known economic hard times. As newlyweds, they rolled pocket change to afford admission to the movies.

Gregg saw Jeff four months before she was introduced to him. They eventually met on a Tuesday and began dating on a Saturday. That's a span of four days—the only days in one and one-half decades in which they have not talked. One has called the other from wherever he or she was in the world. They have, however, spent the vast majority of the time in each other's presence.

And still, Gregg said, the relationship isn't routine.

"He's my best friend," she said. "I just never get tired of him."

"Does he still make you laugh?"

"Every day," she said. "He's funnier at home than he is onstage."

"How did you meet him?"

"I first saw Jeff onstage but I didn't know him," she said. "He was in a contest at the Punch Line here [an Atlanta comedy club]."

Gregg went to the club to see Robert, another stand-up comedian whom she was dating at the time.

Jeff won the contest that night, his first ever onstage. She didn't believe that, as he seemed too polished.

"Had he written his own material?"

"Yes," she said. "And some old jokes. It wasn't that the material was that good, it was him, he was just funny, and I went up to congratulate him afterward and he was real—well—I thought he was stuck-up. Come to find out later, he was just a nervous wreck.

"I really like nice guys," she continued. "And this was not my cup of tea. So that was in May and then I went through the summer and had boyfriends, and then in September I had a girlfriend who was doing amateur comedy. Jeff and I were introduced on a Tuesday and had a date on Saturday."

After one date, Gregg told the other two guys she'd been seeing that she would see them no more. She said she had met Mr. Right.

"You said that after only one date?"

"Yep," she said, laughing. "It was a great date!"

She wanted to backtrack in the history of Jeff and Gregg.

On the Tuesday night when she was officially introduced to Jeff, the two sat down to chat. He obviously intended to be charming. He smiled, joked, and spilled a drink into her lap. Flustered, he fumbled to clean her lap, and spilled a second drink on the place he had just cleaned.

"He was wiping my pants off and he said, 'Oh my goodness,' and it just all dropped, the whole facade and everything of trying to be Mr. Cool, and he said, 'Now you'll never go out with me.'

"I said, 'You haven't asked,'" she recalled. I could hear her smiling on the tape recording.

So Jeff asked her to a party hosted by IBM, his employer at the time.

"And there were all of these people around and he'd be funny and I could tell he was a fun guy at work and everybody loved him," she said. "We were out on this deck, on the first date, and we were just engrossed in conversation and we stopped at one point and it was like something out of a movie. We were so intent on each other that we didn't hear the noise or the company or anything else that was going on."

Gregg used another hackneyed but accurate phrase. She said she and Jeff experienced love at first sight. That must have been true.

Jeff wanted to marry her within three months.

She wasn't ready, and wasn't sure he was either. She was twenty-six. Tension bred friction, there was an argument, and she told him to get out of her life.

Perhaps she merely felt threatened.

She isn't certain why she demanded that he leave, only that she's glad he stayed.

"I think I was a little bit scared," she surmised. "I felt like, 'Okay, if I'm going to really commit to you, if you really love me and I really love you and this is it . . . It's that fight that every couple has early on—that trust fight. It's that one about 'Okay, you have to let me in all the way.'"

And regarding his talent?

She said she knew he was a comic genius almost instantly.

"I said, 'You are a well and nobody's even tapped into it yet. I said that on our first date and it was like he could tell he only showed so much of it. I could tell that it went so deep. There was stuff in there that he didn't even know he had. And he'd always been discouraged. His father was a thirty-year IBM man."

She indicated that Jeff's father was not overly anxious for Jeff to trade the security of a blue-chip company for the uncertain world of show business. Gregg swears she knew Jeff could make it the night of their first date.

"And he swears he knew we were going to get married the night of our first date," she said, laughing again. Gregg was happily astonished at Jeff's penchant toward marriage, given the history of his childhood. His handsome father married six times.

Gregg said that neither she nor Jeff gets overly excited today when Jeff's dad introduces a prospective wife.

"I've met them all and I love his dad and his dad loves women," she said. "I adore his father; Jeff loves his dad. It's not for me to judge; you accept people where they are, and I just love him. I wouldn't want to be married to him."

She said that she has had three new mothers-in-law since her marriage to Jeff.

"I used to get a little frustrated about it," she said.

"Do the ex-wives get together?"

"At Jeff's shows it happens, absolutely," she said, smiling. "We used to joke about having to rent a stadium for the family."

Yet both Jeff and his brother, she stressed again, were extremely domestic and committed to one woman.

Gregg said that the domestic side of their marriage wasn't always mutual. There was a time when Jeff wanted it more than she. It was her idea, for example, for him to leave his secure, three-year-old job at IBM to experiment with a career in comedy.

Tom pointed out that her insistence that Jeff take a career risk was unusual for someone with domestic inclinations like hers.

"I wasn't domestic then," she said.

She said she recalled all the married people she had known, and none seemed happy.

"I used to say, 'I'm not moving to the suburbs.' And talk about diapers," she said. "Now there's nothing I'd rather do. But I would have been resentful if I had done it in my twenties."

"Do you think having children made the difference?" I wanted to know.

"Oh, completely," she said. "It made Jeff's and my relationship. I was afraid it would cause a rift 'cause, you know, your focus changes. All it did was strengthen our relationship."

"Jeff and I go on dates, and he will tell the two girls, 'I'm going to kiss your mama tonight.' They'll giggle. The other day he told them that and the oldest one said, 'Okay, wait and take your time and when she's not expecting it, just surprise her.' And he told the little one he was going to kiss me and she said, 'Do it now, Daddy, do it now!'"

Gregg said she thinks she did not fear picking Jeff's show business pursuits over corporate security, because she knew that money and happiness were not synonymous.

"I had made money in my early twenties with a company in Denver," she recalled. She had sold insurance.

"I had all of this *stuff*," she said. "I was driving a Mercedes at twenty-one and owned a condo so I had accomplished things materially—things that I knew did not bring me happiness. My father has always been successful and he's made a great deal of money. But he always said, 'You really need to enjoy what you're doing and never stress the material end of it.' So I wasn't afraid for Jeff to quit his job. I always knew if we had to make money, we could. I could always go sell insurance and he could go get a job with IBM."

On December 31, 1984, Jeff walked out of IBM to try his hand, firmly in Gregg's, in the entertainment industry.

He soon had to take a job as a Kelly Girl, working at a temporary employment service in Atlanta.

Later, he went on the road, driving from comedy club to comedy club. Gregg worked as a milk salesperson for an Atlanta dairy, and met Jeff on weekends wherever he was playing.

"I would take a bus to someplace and then drive back with him on Sunday after the Saturday night show," she said. "I would get up on Monday mornings and go to the dairy."

She had a routine.

She'd get off work on Friday night and drive her car to the Greyhound station. She'd take the bus to meet Jeff, whose Friday night show had usually adjourned. So she would wait for him to pick her up in the wee hours of a weekend morning inside a hollow and dank public bus station. She sat alone, waiting for her man while turning from the stares of drunks and derelicts.

"Weren't you afraid?"

"I was too naive to be afraid," she said. "I never had a bad experience."

She said that she firmly believes that God was watching over her.

She and Jeff would spend Saturday together, and she would critique his Saturday night show. They'd drive back to Atlanta on Sunday. En route, they would discuss his performance. He took her criticism seriously.

"Absolutely," she said. "I told him to hold his head up and look at the audience because sometimes he looked at the floor. I gave him a critique early on that fortunately he didn't take. I said, 'You're going to have to lose your southern accent.' I'd grown up around theater. I told him he'd never be able to work in New York or Los Angeles with that accent."

Jeff says that when people in Hollywood hear him speak they instantly deduct one hundred points from his IQ.

Once back in Atlanta, she worked nights making industrial films and television commercials. She had been a theater major before dropping out of college, and at one time had her own theatrical aspirations. Ultimately, they took a backseat to his. She insists she was meant to be his helpmate, the woman behind the man in front of the masses.

"So you were the family breadwinner in the early days?"

"Right," she said. "I say that I put him through medical school. When I met him my mother said, 'Oh, you're going to take care of another one, are you?' I had a tendency to do that. But I said, 'No, this one is different Mom, I swear.'"

Jeff is as famous for his "You might be a redneck if . . ." routines as Jack Benny was for frugality, or Rodney Dangerfield is for "I don't get no respect."

"You might be a redneck if your dad walks you to school because he's in the same grade," is one of thousands of "redneck" jokes Jeff has written in twelve books.

Gregg remembers the routine's inception.

"He was on the road and he called me and he said, 'Do you think this is funny?' He had two or three of the redneck jokes."

And the ball was rolling.

Later, when they were driving home in the middle of the night after a show, she said they became "punchy" with fatigue. Jeff started rattling off the preface, "You might be a redneck if . . ." Sometimes he finished the line, sometimes she did, and sometimes they just thought. But they came up with ten punch lines. She calls them the "original ten." They're framed on the envelope on which they were written.

The list grew to one hundred, and Gregg sent them to various book publishers. Each rejected the jokes, except for Longstreet Press in Atlanta.

"He came home and said, 'They're going to buy the book and they're going to give me $1,500 up front,'" she recalled. "We thought we had hit the lottery. I mean, we were screaming and yelling. That remains his biggest break. I mean, the redneck thing is the basis for his whole career."

She was twenty-nine.

Gregg put a notepad by Jeff's bedstand. Jeff would often awaken in the night to write a one-liner.

Gregg eventually toured with Jeff, and sold his joke books at the back of the comedy rooms.

"I'd stand there and take people's money and tell them his name," she said. "That went on, like, through '89. At that point I had quit my job, so I was going on the road with him."

They had by then been married long enough to be more than newlyweds, but not long enough to be an old couple. The recollections of their wedding are themselves a hilarious routine.

Jeff had won a comedy contest whose first prize was a chance to perform at Dangerfield's in New York City. Fare was not included.

Gregg's mother worked for Delta Airlines, and finagled a ticket for Gregg and Jeff to the Big Apple. Jeff had never been there before.

He didn't work Dangerfield's the first night he arrived. Broke, he supplemented his income by playing smaller clubs around New York and in New Jersey. That meant riding a subway at night, something else he had never done.

He was paid one hundred dollars for his first show. Fearful that he might be robbed, he pretended to be drunk and mentally ill while riding the late-night train to his shabby Times Square hotel. He thought no one would mess with anyone who was disturbed. He pulled out his shirt, messed his hair, and babbled loudly.

He entered his hotel, where he frightened Gregg, who thought he'd been mugged.

Jeff had only twenty-four hours off that week from metropolitan New York one-nighters. Jeff and Gregg decided to spend the day getting married. The day barely contained enough time.

They found out that they did not need a blood

test in order to buy a marriage license, and thought the procedure would therefore be complication-free. They took a subway to the courthouse to buy the license and stood in line with a fifteen-year-old girl. She could not speak English. She could not tell Jeff and Gregg that she was pregnant. She also could not tell them when her water broke.

Gregg couldn't recognize the girl's language. She saw a black man, and hoped he wasn't American. She also hoped he could understand the girl. He couldn't either.

People who appeared to be members of the girl's family soon gathered around. Perhaps they weren't family at all. Perhaps they just spoke the same mysterious language. No paramedics came, as there was no need. The people carried the girl giving birth out the door. Neither Gregg nor Jeff understood if anyone was directing the imminent mother to push.

She never got her marriage license, but Gregg and Jeff got theirs. But they didn't get married—not until the next day.

"That's because the Lord moves in mysterious ways," Gregg said, again smiling.

"We were looking for a justice of the peace and couldn't find one," she said. "So we started calling churches and we said, 'We have only one day that we can get married.'"

"And nobody would marry us," she said. "And we kept going through the phone book through churches and we were down to 'U' for Unitarian.

"This Reverend Leonard answered the phone," she said.

"Can you marry us?" he was asked.

"Sure," he said. "It will be two hundred and fifty dollars. One hundred for me and one hundred and fifty for the chapel."

Jeff and Gregg would have had to borrow money for the ceremony.

Jeff told the minister to forget the chapel.

"Do you have a garden or something?" he asked.

"I'm across the street from Central Park," said the clergyman. "Would you like to get married in the park?"

They consented.

In the absence of a rehearsal banquet the couple opted for lunch at Tavern on the Green.

The preacher, Jeff, Gregg, and a Central Park groundskeeper attended the ceremony. The groundskeeper wasn't invited, but when he sensed that a wedding was transpiring on the very spot he had just swept, he pleaded with the preacher to prevent the throwing of rice. Then he asked Jeff and Gregg personally.

His pleas fell on deaf ears. Rice was the only thing affordable that gave the proceedings a remote resemblance to a traditional wedding.

Rob Bartlett, a friend in New York, showed up with his pregnant wife. She spoke English, and her water didn't break throughout the entire blessed event.

The groundskeeper, who spoke broken English, was by then begging everyone in the paltry party not to throw rice.

Rob cut a deal with the guy. He told him he'd give him twenty dollars and that he could be in the wedding pictures if they could throw rice.

The man agreed, and it's a good thing. Jeff and Gregg had passionately determined to have rice thrown, so much so that they were personally ready to throw it at the groundskeeper.

There is one Instamatic picture of the "ceremony." It contains the happy couple, the minister, whose first name they've forgotten, and the groundskeeper, whose name they never knew.

There were more one-nighters. The clubs got nicer, the distance between them shorter. By 1990 Jeff Foxworthy had released four editions of his "redneck" books, and had worked his way up to the Comedy Magic Club in Los Angeles.

One night, one of the customers was Jay Leno.

Johnny Carson was still the full-time *Tonight Show* host, Jay the regular guest host. The guest host asked Jeff to be his guest comedian.

"It was 1990 and we had just moved to L.A.," Gregg said.

"So that trip was wonderful?" Tom asked.

"It was awful," she replied.

Jeff hadn't wanted to move to Los Angeles, as he knew he would miss his Atlanta friends and lifestyle. He didn't then, nor does he now, see himself as a California guy. Gregg argued that he had to go for the brass ring, contending that if he did not, he would wonder for the rest of his life what would have happened. She insisted that the haunting curiosity would be unbearable.

Jeff was still not convinced. So Gregg said that she wanted to renew her own show business ambitions, and that the Los Angeles move would be for her as much as for him. That wasn't true. She also told Jeff they would move to Los Angeles for only six months, and afterward return to Atlanta if nothing had happened in their careers.

"In my mind," she said, "there was no deadline. But he thought he was going to get to move back to Atlanta in six months."

The childless couple took off for a new life in a new car that Gregg had bought with savings from various freelance television commercials and other random jobs. They packed everything portable along with two cats and themselves.

"The trip was miserable, miserable," she kept insisting. "The night before we left we had Jeff's dad over with wife number four," she said. "They had words."

She indicated that the words evolved into a full-blown argument that went on until after midnight. Jeff and Gregg just wanted them to leave their house so they could leave for California.

Atlanta never has fog. The morning the Foxworthys embarked for California the entire city was enshrouded. Atlanta is one of the fastest-growing cities in the United States. Traffic and gridlock are one. On this morning, no one could see the car that was blocking them. The couple got as far as Gadsden, Alabama, where they pulled over for gasoline. Afterward, when they pulled out, someone plowed into the side of their new car.

Jeff didn't think the trip was going overly well so far. They got out and exchanged information with the other driver, and conversation was difficult. They couldn't hear above the driving rain. They couldn't wait for the comfort of a motel—rest from the night of parental arguing and day of rainfall and wreckage.

They untied their bags from the top of the dented car.

They dragged the new waterproof luggage into their motel, opened it, and dipped for their floating clothes. The luggage was indeed waterproof. It hadn't let a drop of water escape.

"Everything was soaked, the cats were screaming, the car was wrecked, and we were exhausted," Gregg said.

Jeff was certain that the trip was not going well.

"Do you suppose God is trying to tell us something?" he asked Gregg.

She knew that a lot of people would have turned back. She didn't say if Jeff would have been one of them, had it not been for her. She didn't have to.

Rhonda Adkins.
*Photograph
by Tony Phipps.
Used by permission.*

Rhonda and Trace Adkins on their wedding day in 1997.
Photograph by Allen Griggs.

Kix and Barbara Brooks, 1997.
Family photograph.

Barbara Brooks and
Angel, 1993.
Family photograph.

Kix, Eric, Barbara, and Molly holding Hillary Clinton's cat. *Family photograph.*

Sandy Brooks 1983.
Family photograph.

Garth and Sandy Brooks. Photograph by Judy Mock. *Used by permission.*

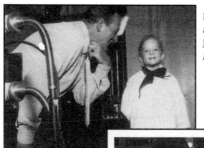

Lisa Hartman Black, age seven, with John Wayne. *Family photograph.*

Clint and Lisa Hartman Black. Photograph by Judy Mock. *Used by permission.*

Clint and Lisa Hartman Black on their wedding day. *Family photograph.*

Kim Campbell, age four.
Family photograph.

Shannon, Kim, Glen, Ashley, and
Cal Campbell in Israel, 1996.
Family photograph.

Glen and Kim Campbell, 1981.
Family photograph.

Tish Cyrus, three
years old.
Family photograph.

Tish and Billy Ray Cyrus with
(clockwise from left) Destiny, Cody,
Brandi, Trace, and Braison.
Family photograph.

Tish and Billy Ray Cyrus in 1996.
*Photograph by
Morrison/Wulffraat/Retna.*

Janine Dunn and
Johnny Cash, 1984.
Family photograph.

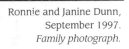

Ronnie and Janine Dunn,
September 1997.
Family photograph.

Theresa Haggard in 1987.
Family photograph.

Theresa Haggard with her father, Erv Lane, on her wedding day, September 11, 1993. *Family photograph.*

Merle and Theresa Haggard in 1997 during the filming of *Tales Out of Luck* at Willie Nelson's ranch in Austin, Texas. *Family photograph.*

Denise Jackson, cheerleading captain, Newman High School Cougars, fall 1977. *Family photograph.*

Alan and Denise Jackson, December 15, 1979. *Family photograph.*

Nancy Jones at age thirty.
Family photograph.

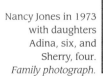

Nancy Jones in 1973
with daughters
Adina, six, and
Sherry, four.
Family photograph.

Nancy Jones with
grandchildren Cameron
Estes and Breann Hohimer.
Family photograph.

George and Nancy
Jones in 1996.
*Photograph by
Judy Mock.
Used by
permission.*

Sharon PayCheck with son Jonathan "Bo" PayCheck in 1996. *Family photograph.*

Johnny and Sharon PayCheck in 1972. *Family photograph.*

Johnny and Sharon PayCheck on a cruise in 1997. *Family photograph.*

Charley and Rozene Pride, 1994. *Family photograph.*

Wanda Rogers, age eleven.
Family photograph.

Wanda and Kenny Rogers on their wedding day in 1997.
Family photograph.

Wanda and Kenny
Rogers in 1996.
Family photograph.

The marriage license for the second wedding of Mr. and Mrs. Hank Williams. *Courtesy of the Robert Gentry Collection.*

Hank and Billy Jean Williams at their second wedding in October 1952. *Courtesy of the Robert Gentry Collection.*

The grave of Hank Williams in Montgomery, Alabama. *Courtesy of the Robert Gentry Collection.*

Johnny Horton, far right, behind Billy Jean Horton.
Courtesy of the Robert Gentry Collection.

Johnny Horton with Billy Jean and children in 1956.
Courtesy of the Robert Gentry Collection.

Arch and Wynonna Kelley on their first date, 1993.
Photograph by Alan L. Mayor.

Arch and Wynonna on
their wedding day,
January 21, 1996.
Family photograph.

Arch and Wynonna with
their children, Gracie (left)
and Elijah (right), and Santa
Claus at Christmas in 1996.
Family photograph.

They drove the next day and made it to a city beyond the Midwest. Tired and still damp, they anticipated a new night in a new hotel. They had both—with a new problem. They stayed under a room where the man above was a cowboy who had taken up tap dancing—in boots—all night. They let the cats cry, and the bawling eventually became so loud that it overpowered the stomping.

Jeff was eventually offered another network show before he was offered *The Jeff Foxworthy Show*. He and the producers had creative differences. So he refunded the advance he was paid, although he wasn't legally obliged to do so.

Gregg said no one in Hollywood could believe he did that. Jeff was in a new city, but he had brought his old convictions. His morality wouldn't let him keep money for a job he didn't complete.

By 1995, his namesake show was written for him. He had appeared on *The Tonight Show* several times, had won a Grammy award for a comedy album, and had continued to churn out a comedy book annually. More awards followed. He recorded a novelty record with country music superstar Alan Jackson.

For years, it had been Jeff and Gregg against the world. Now they had conquered the world, at least as far as it stretched into show business.

The Jeff Foxworthy Show was canceled after two seasons. Jeff was thrilled, Gregg said, as that meant he could move back to his beloved Atlanta. Gregg said Jeff's only remorse stemmed from the unemployment faced by hairdressers, makeup personnel, and others who worked on his show. He helped many of them get jobs.

Jeff was subsequently offered his own talk show, another television series, and a motion picture. He turned all of it down.

"Because he doesn't want to live in California," said Gregg. "He wanted to come home to Atlanta."

As of this writing, the couple is building a larger house, and fondly looking back on old times while they are still young.

"What's Jeff going to do back in Atlanta?"

"He's going to take his little girls to school," Gregg said, again smiling. "He's going to work on his golf swing. He'll be giving his Christian testimony for the first time next month. He's doing another comedy album. He'll continue to write books, and do comedy on weekends. We are now the celebrity chairmen of the Duke Medical Center Children's Classic."

"He can retire if he wants, right?"

"Absolutely, we have saved our money," she said. "And being back home, he's happier than he's ever been. He sings, he dances, he's the boy I married. His neck doesn't creak anymore."

I recalled the old adage about how you can take the boy out of the country, but you can't take the country out of the boy.

And then I thought about how you can't take the love out of some couples.

"Well," it was suggested, teasingly, "perhaps Jeff and you can eventually return to L.A. to pursue your acting career. Why not play a joke on him and tell him that's what you want to do?"

"No thanks," she said, once again smiling. "I think I'd rather keep my marriage."

9

*I met Mrs. Merle (Theresa) Haggard in 1991 when
her husband was on a concert tour with my husband,
George, and the late Conway Twitty. The three men
worked many shows together, and the wives saw each
other at some of the programs.*

*I never really became close to Theresa. She lives in
California, and I in Tennessee. I run into her once a year,
if that often.*

*But first impressions are the most lasting, and I
vividly remember our first meeting. Merle and Theresa
had invited us over to their bus. We stepped on board as
Merle was seated and Theresa emerged from the state-
room, slender and blonde with a glowing personality.
Merle and she received us warmly.*

Mrs. Merle Haggard had poured her heart out, had
answered every question directly and honestly. The conversation perhaps had been embarrassing to her, but she
eventually laughed and said the talk had been a good
experience. That's how the conversation ended.

But it wasn't over.

She called within twenty-four hours.

"I wasn't really quite honest with you yesterday," she said.

Pause.

"It's about the drugs."

"Okay, I asked if you had ever seen your husband use drugs."

"No," she said. "It's me."

"You?"

"And I have, and I had a problem with it," she continued. She said she'd been addicted to stimulants, and that Merle had helped her get off the stuff.

"And the only reason I was able to get off it was because Merle helped me, and also so did the Big Guy," she said. "I was healed by Holy Communion several times a day."

She spoke in spurts, the way people do when they're confessing something that makes them uncomfortable.

She said she'd been drug-free for four months.

Not much time? Perhaps. But before that she'd been using several times a day for years, and had frequently gone as many as three days without sleep, propelled by the crystallized amphetamines ("crank") inside her system. Four months seemed like a giant step toward healing.

"It's been bothering me since I said no to you [yesterday]," she said.

Actually, Tom explained, she had not been asked if she had used drugs. She had been asked if she'd seen her husband abuse drugs.

It didn't matter. She'd wanted to come clean, and called across 2,500 miles to do so.

She had begun her drug use innocently enough, taking prescription drugs to alleviate a respiratory condition. Her condition improved, and she no longer needed the drugs, but she wanted them. So she substituted street drugs.

"I had taken the medicine and it had made me feel wired," she said. "When I got to where I could actually breathe and didn't need the medicine anymore, I went to the street stuff. I had been on it [prescription medicine] a good portion of my life."

As she spoke, she had been drug-free for one third of her thirty-seventh year.

"Did your usage make for disruptions in your marriage?" Tom asked.

"Yes," she said, after more hesitation. "I got to a point where I knew if I didn't stop I'd lose Merle. Maybe not, but I had that fear."

She is his sixth wife.

"But now, with the Lord's help and Merle's, I'm free of that [addiction]."

It's hard to believe you kicked it without going through rehabilitation therapy, I thought.

"That's why I say the Holy Communion and Merle's faith in me," she said. "There was nothing here on Earth that could have helped me. Every time I felt like I needed to turn to the drug, I would do the Holy Communion." She meant that she prayed intensely, and she called the Holy Communion the body and blood of Jesus Christ.

"Jesus left it for us when He died to claim healing of sin and sickness. I remember watching this on Gene Scott's channel."

Dr. Gene Scott is a television minister whose program is seen in California, Theresa's home, and elsewhere. She said that she and Merle used to watch Scott for two and three days without sleep while strung out on drugs.

"What would you say was one of the most dramatic disruptions of your marriage or personal happiness from using that drug?" Tom asked, in search of a specific example.

"Almost losing Merle," she said again, and never made reference to any particular clash between them.

"Did he say to you, 'Either quit or I'm going to leave you'?"

"No, but I just knew that he would," she said. "It wasn't fair to him. He wasn't seeing the real me, and I wasn't either."

She said she contracted a diagnosed disease similar to mononucleosis during the throes of her drug consumption. She said she was healed of it at the same time she was healed of her drug use.

"I've been healed," she said. "There was a time when I couldn't even get up."

Broadcast and published reports have cited Merle as the drug abuser in the family.

"No," she said. "No. I mean, he was at one time, but he got off and then he helped me."

• • •

Theresa was born in Elk Grove, California, just south of Sacramento. She is the oldest of five children. Her father was an engineer, her mother worked in an almond packaging plant.

She didn't talk much about her childhood, and said that her first marriage didn't work out. The first divorce for most Nashville wives is a gimme.

While she was separated from husband number one, and while she was even contemplating returning to him in South Dakota, her mother said that she was going to a show with the Maddox Brothers and Sister Rose, also starring Merle Haggard.

Theresa had never heard of any entertainers named Maddox or Merle. "Up until then I was a rock-'n'-roller," she said. "I liked the Rolling Stones and Fleetwood Mac—you know, the seventies era of rock 'n' roll."

But she wound up accompanying her mother to Silverthorn, a California resort Merle owned on Lake Shasta at the time.

"I met one of Merle's guitar players and stayed," Theresa said. "I told my mom I'd catch a bus home the next day."

She went with the guitarist to his quarters and the telephone rang. It was Merle. He wanted the guitarist to come to his room and wanted him to bring Theresa, whom he had seen with the guitarist after the show. The guitarist declined, but Merle kept calling. And Merle was his employer.

"The guitar player finally said that we were going over to Merle's, but that I needed to watch him," she recalled.

"Why?" she asked the guitarist.

"You just need to watch him," the guitarist repeated.

"I don't know why Merle wanted us to come over," she said.

"And so we went over there and it was really the first time I got to meet Merle and my face turned three shades of red and Merle kept looking at me and stuff," she remembered.

"You could feel yourself blushing?"

"Oh God, I felt myself on fire," she said. "I had seen his show the previous night and we stayed there the next day and the guitar player asked if I could come along on the next tour with him," she said. "Merle said that was fine for a few days, and told me I could ride with the band to their next shows in Las Vegas. And so we got to Las Vegas and the first show, there were two shows, and the guitar player and I were just friends going together—not really going together, just going to the shows together, and then Merle, in between shows, asked us to come to his room."

Once inside, Merle asked the guitarist to go fetch something from the band's tour bus, Theresa said.

When he returned to Merle's room, he found the door locked. Merle and Theresa were inside and would not open the door.

The man continued to knock loudly, to no avail. He then went to his own room and telephoned Merle. Merle answered, and told the musician to go away, Theresa said.

The guitarist is no longer with the show. Theresa said his departure, years after the incident, had nothing to do with Merle's blockade.

"So the guitar player couldn't get inside?" Tom asked. "Did you stay with Merle that night?"

"I stayed with him throughout the whole next— all thirty days—of his tour. Yeah, we were together, and then we started seeing each other, and I eventually moved up to Merle's house."

"Had his previous wife been singer/songwriter Leona Williams?" Theresa was asked.

"Debbie Parrot, Parret, I think," she said.

"And hadn't she been his maid at one time?"

"Yes."

"And they were married for how long?"

"I don't know, I would say a couple of years, maybe," she answered.

She then named the women to whom Merle was married before he married the maid.

"So to your knowledge he's had five former wives?"

"Well, I'm his sixth."

"He doesn't exactly have a solid marital track record," Tom pointed out.

"I didn't even think about that," she said. "I was in love with him and I didn't even think about that. I saw a man I really admired, and I still do."

"What is it about him that you admire?" Tom asked.

"His giving personality," she said. "I also admire his faith in God. The way he carries himself. He's a great father. Our daughter was in our wedding. Both children were born before we got married. We've been married for four years," she said.

"And you've been dating for eleven?"

"Right."

"Where did you get married?"

"Right here in our yard," she said. "No—when we had our second baby. Well, actually, our first baby was still young and we were living on the lake on a houseboat. We were worried about [the baby] falling into the water and those kinds of things. So we decided to live on land and we moved up here on Merle's ranch in Palo Cedro.

"We lived about three years on the lake and it was great," she went on. "It was a two-story houseboat and it was fully equipped like a house and it had a Jacuzzi upstairs, it had household things, you know—flushing toilets, all that kind of stuff. It was very nice."

Theresa is today thirty-eight, Merle sixty-one. She said their age difference is no problem, and said they have had an exciting sex life. Their children are eight and five.

Theresa said she would like to be involved in Merle's career more than she is, but can't travel with him as much as she'd like because of their children. She said she thinks Merle lived in Nashville for a couple of years before his marriage to her, but she isn't entirely sure.

She appeared to know little more about his past than what he had volunteered.

"Do you have any hobbies or interests that are independent of Merle Haggard?" she was asked.

"Yes," she said. "I'm a health nut. I love anything healthy. I'm more into trying to help others with their health."

"Do you try to involve Merle in these things?"

"Oh yeah," she said. "He's a very good patient. He smoked Camels for forty years and then he finally—he quit. Quit cold turkey. We went and got hypnotized, and it didn't really kick in. Then one day, I guess he couldn't get a fresh cigarette, and he got tired of always smoking Camels. And plus not being able to breathe was really a factor when he had me on top of him."

She was referring to her constant urging for Merle to stop smoking.

She spoke as plans were being negotiated for a motion picture about Merle's life. Its executive producer would be Robert Duvall, its screenwriter Billy Bob Thornton, both Academy Award winners. Theresa said she would like to be in the movie, but wasn't sure she would be, since she was not an actress.

"But give me a shot at it, and I'll sure give it hell."

During the previous two weeks, the *National Enquirer* had carried two articles about Merle's allegedly dramatic former character failings. The allegations, hurled by his son Marty, had been picked up by the mainstream press. The Nashville music community was buzzing.

There was tabloid fare about Merle's being an alleged wife beater. The son claimed that, when he was a child, Merle had once locked him inside a sweltering car trunk in the California heat. He said that his father had forced him to sit in a bathtub with live catfish, and claimed the fish ate pieces of him. There were also stories from the son about his father's supposed sexual shenanigans while on tour. The son claimed that his dad had paid for tour prostitutes with whom the son celebrated one of his teenage birthdays.

Theresa not only doesn't believe the allegations, she even refused to read them.

"I threw away the second article," she said. "I read part of it and I didn't read the first one, because I know my husband and from what I've heard [about the articles] it's just, you know, the battery and beatings, this is not the Merle Haggard I know."

She said she didn't believe the reports.

"Has there ever been domestic violence in your marriage?" Tom asked.

"No, no," she insisted. "All we have in our marriage is love."

"Do you believe the previous wives who said Merle was violent with them?"

"No, he's not that type. He's the most tender man I've ever met."

As an example of Merle's tenderness, she cited one of his surprises for her. About four months before the 1989 birth of Genessa, their first child, Merle told Theresa he would be leaving their home daily for a few months. He and Theresa were still living on the houseboat. He told Theresa she could not ask where he was going, that she would simply have to trust him.

Her baby was born on December 23. The day after Christmas, on the way home from the hospital, Merle drove Theresa and his new daughter along a back road to an old cabin he owned. Theresa could not see the front. Once inside the yard, Theresa could see that Merle had expanded and remodeled the place.

"It was beautiful," she said.

He had been preparing a home for the family during his four-month absence. The family still lives there to this day.

Merle had also bought Theresa and their new baby clothes to wear home from the hospital, as well as an entire new wardrobe for Theresa. She said he selects all of her clothing.

She said that much of her marriage is spent in Bible reading, adding that she and Merle study the Scriptures together.

"Before I met Merle I was raised Catholic," she said. "I really didn't learn a lot about the Catholic religion. I skimmed over the top, you know, and I didn't understand a lot of what they said until I met Merle. He gave me a Bible and then he started explaining to me and I've learned most of my stuff from him."

Minutes before the interview, she had been reading the Book of Revelations about the second coming of Christ, she said.

Merle has been described as self-destructive for years. He has conceded his heavy drinking during his youth and twenties and told Ralph Emery during a nationally televised show that he once thought he had a problem with cocaine abuse. He has undergone dramatic mood swings, and has told reporters about his bouts with depression and sadness.

Tom asked Theresa to explain Merle's self-destructiveness, but she couldn't because she denied that he was self-destructive. The extent of his self-destructiveness, she said, is that he worries too much about other people. But, she insisted, that wasn't really self-destructiveness, and Merle really has no self-destructive qualities.

"Was he self-destructive before you met him?" Tom asked.

"I don't know," she said. "I really don't. I didn't know Merle Haggard. I didn't even know who he was before I met him."

Merle has recorded forty-one number-one country songs, more than any other living country music artist. He has been a keeper of the flame of traditional country music, no matter what the popular trends. He has consistently recorded music because he liked it and for no other reason, including commercial acceptability.

In 1971, in the wake of his explosive 1960s popularity, he told Capitol Records that he wanted to record a gospel album and record it live inside four of America's smallest churches, including the Nashville Rescue Mission for transients. The label balked, and pointed out that other country artists were trying to incorporate symphony orchestras into their recordings, and that his proposal was behind the times. Gospel albums recorded in a studio didn't sell, he was told. The idea of recording one inside four obscure churches was unthinkable.

Merle nonetheless recorded the critically acclaimed *Land of Many Churches*, and got his way about doing one side at the Nashville Rescue Mission.

Theresa said she had familiarized herself with Merle's music, but indicated little knowledge of his background. He had told her things about his personal life, but had passed on talking about his legendary career.

"Did you know that in the 1970s he was billed as 'the poet of the common man'?" she was asked.

She didn't recall.

"Have you heard about the time a disc jockey was supposed to introduce him as the 'poet of the common man,' but mistakenly called him the 'poor old common man'?"

She howled at the story. She had not heard it.

"Have you ever asked [about his past]?"

"I didn't ask," she said. "I remember in nineteen-something, I remember it was probably one of the first times I'd heard anything on the radio by him and [it was] 'Okie from Muskogee' but I didn't put the two together. I didn't know who Merle Haggard was, but I knew I liked that song."

"Do you think Merle can be unpredictable?"

She didn't say.

"Does he ever surprise you?"

"He always surprises me," she said.

"Can you give an example of the most recent surprise?"

She explained that Merle had gotten permission from their county government to name a road that crosses their land after her. He had posted signs along the road, and each bore her name.

"What's one of the most endearing things you remember about your years with Merle Haggard?"

"Well, having our two children," she said. "I mean, he wasn't in the room with me the first time, but the second time, that was something, just right after he was born, Merle was holding the baby.

"He was there when my mother died, and he sang at her funeral—just him and the guitar.

"Another memory I have, probably our best memories, is fishing nude in the moonlight."

"Did you catch anything when you were nude in the moonlight?"

"Yeah," she said. "I did. I caught a big one."

I'm not sure she meant a fish.

10

Alan and Denise Jackson were married when this chapter was written in October 1997. I learned in February 1998 that they had separated. I was simultaneously astonished and brokenhearted. The two reconciled in May. They are currently living happily together.

* * *

On January 13, 1990, Alan Jackson released "Here in the Real World," his second song for Arista Records. His first, "Blue Blooded Woman," had risen only to number forty-five on the *Billboard* country chart, and to number forty-three on *Radio and Records*. Had "Real" not become the number-three song in the nation, Alan might not have been given a third chance to score major recording success. That would have depended on Arista, whose executives were aware that the country music industry was very competitive, with many young acts waiting in the wings.

But "Real" spent twenty-six weeks on the *Bill-*

board survey. Alan had a number of career dreams, including meeting George Jones. Alan said George had been his musical ideal for most of his young life. In April 1990, Debbie Doebler, who handles Alan's and George's money, arranged a meeting between the show-business veteran and newcomer, and their wives. We dined at the Cock of the Walk, a catfish restaurant at Opryland.

Mrs. Alan (Denise) Jackson was pregnant with Mattie, the first of three daughters. George likes to eat early, and he likes his privacy. So Debbie arranged for the restaurant to open early, and we dined with the place to ourselves. Denise was one of those people I instantly liked. To use a shopworn adjective, she was "sweet." We became more than associates, as an actual friendship quickly evolved. She sent gifts when my two grandchildren were born, and remembers their birthdays. She and Alan came to George's sixty-fourth birthday party, three days before a heart attack resulted in his triple bypass. She called regularly about George's well-being. Alan has gone on to win a bushel-basketful of awards—George calls him the keeper of the flame of country music. I don't think there has been one wife in Nashville who has stood more firmly behind her man during his lean times than Denise Jackson. When Tom Carter and I decided to write this book, Denise's name was among the first to surface as someone we wanted to participate.

• • •

A million-dollar romance started with a penny.

The former Denise Jackson, sixteen, was sitting in the Dairy Queen in her hometown of Newnan, Georgia, after church on a Sunday evening in 1976. The ice cream parlor was the franchised hangout for teenagers. There was not even a McDonald's in Newnan at the time. The place was for the good kids in semirural, west-central Georgia. Denise had noticed a slender, handsome blond boy who belonged to another church, but came to the "in" place on Sunday nights after his own services were dismissed. She had actually seen him years earlier when he played with her brother, but she was inattentive to boys in those days. She didn't know his last name. (It was the same as hers.)

To this day, neither Alan nor Denise Jackson has fully researched their ancestry. Alan was her escort during high school homecoming ceremonies. Some observers thought they were brother and sister.

"Both of our fathers did grow up in western Georgia," she said. "So I'm afraid if we researched too far we might find out that we're related [as blood relatives]."

On that long-ago Sunday after church, Alan sat next to her, made small talk, tapped her interest, and without invitation or provocation, dropped a penny down her blouse.

He kidded about retrieving the copper, then left the restaurant. Within perhaps fifteen minutes, so did she.

She got in her mother's car, turned on the ignition, drove two blocks—and nearly jumped through the roof.

Alan Jackson, the flirtatious and nice boy, leapt from the back floorboard where he had been hiding. He never got his penny, just a ride around town while Denise caught her breath. Three and a half years later he caught a wife.

Actually, it wasn't exactly that easy. Alan called for a date; she said no. He waited for a few months before asking again, and she accepted.

"Why did you wait so long to go out with him?" I asked.

"I don't know," Denise said, "I was really just not that impressed with him and I thought I just really don't want to go out with him."

She said he looked goofy.

"Maybe it was the penny throwing," I suggested.

"It could have been. But maybe it was this new hairstyle—parting his hair in the middle."

Denise, a girl reared around white picket fences rather than neon signs, married her high school sweetheart. Alan describes their economic backgrounds as blue-collar. Each worked odd jobs in high school, in college, and even after their marriage. They wed on December 15, 1979, inside a church where about two hundred guests heard Alan sing "The Wedding Song," an untraditional version by Pat Terry.

"I remember Alan telling people he was more nervous about singing that he was about getting married," Denise said, laughing.

Their ceremony, like their courtship, had the innocence of a 1950s situation comedy.

"We'd have a fight," Denise said, "and he'd ask somebody out, so I'd go out again with the quarterback. It was silly."

Denise's laughter at their romantic history is audio nostalgia for me. I love to hear people talk about how they fell in love.

"It was Christmas Eve," Denise said, a gleam returning to her eye. "We were at my parents' house and everybody had gone to bed and we [Alan and she] decided to open our presents. We had not even talked about marriage. I mean, golly, we were just kids. I had started my first year of college and I was sitting on Mother's living room floor and he was getting that little box out and it scared me to death. I mean, I thought, Surely this is going to be earrings. And I will never forget opening that box and seeing that half-carat round engagement ring. It shocked me to death. I just thought, I'm only eighteen years old. Why is he giving this to me?

"And when I opened it," she continued, "he said, 'Will you marry me?'

"I just sat there. I didn't say a word. I mean, for two or three minutes I didn't say a word. And finally he said, 'You don't have to answer me yet.' And so the shock wore off, and in a few minutes I said yes."

She told him she wanted to wait awhile. One year later, on the virtual anniversary of their engagement, they were wed.

She still has the half-carat engagement ring,

despite a ten-carat masterpiece she now wears, and she still occasionally wears her original wedding band.

But she didn't for a while.

After getting her larger ring, she temporarily hid her smaller one. She forgot where. She searched frantically for days, and ultimately feared that a member of her domestic staff might have taken the ring. Then she remembered having hid it in a sock drawer. She was later relieved that she had made no false accusations.

"I would give up all my jewelry," she said. "Alan is so wonderful to give me so many wonderful things, but that little ring is still—I'd give up all my jewelry to keep it."

Denise's siblings are her twin brother, Danny, and an older sister, Jane. Alan is the only boy in a family of five children. The wealth, long in coming, is sizable.

Yet Denise never forgot what it was like to see how the other half—the rich half—lived. She watched for years through a television screen or colorful catalog. So for Christmas 1996 she gave her mother a mink coat, and Alan did the same for his.

"And my mom opened it and she was just prancing around like a teenager and was just thrilled," Denise recalled, tears in her eyes. "We even got her little mink earmuffs. Well, my sister-in-law said, 'Nell, where are you going to go in your mink coat?'

"'I'm going to Ryan Steak House,' Mom said."

Ryan Steak House may have replaced the Dairy

Queen as the "in" restaurant in Newnan. There isn't a lot of cold weather in Georgia. But Denise's mom wore her coat when it was forty degrees, and Denise was proud of her for it.

Denise Jackson is one show business wife who is, foremost, a wife. The show business is secondary.

She jokes that she was finally attracted to Alan, two years older than she, because he had a 1955 restored Thunderbird. Twelve years and a few million records after they were married, Alan owned seventeen cars, according to an article in a national magazine. One Christmas morning Denise gave him another.

"That car," he told her, "looks just like the 1955 Thunderbird I built in high school," he said.

"It is!" she said.

Alan Jackson, who by then had performed before millions in live and television audiences, wept unashamedly. Denise's gift was the culmination of a multimonth trace of the car's ownership. It was the first car he'd owned, the first in which they'd dated, and the last they would ever think about selling.

Alan had restored the car in high school. He sold it to raise cash to make the down payment on his and Denise's first house. Alan initially bought the car for $2,000. It became a collector's item, particularly after his meticulous improvements. Denise bought it back for $24,000. It's now museum quality.

Denise impresses me as a very determined person. She's determined, for example, that nothing gets in the way of the family time that she and Alan share with their three daughters. On nights when he's not on the concert trail, she sees to it that all telephones in the house are turned off. Alan happily complies. The music business runs twenty-four hours a day in Nashville. Some of the biggest deals are made after dark. If one is offered on behalf of Alan Jackson, the dealmakers simply have to wait until morning, no matter who they are, no matter how much the money.

Then, like the all-American family they are, the Jackson household arises at 6:00 A.M. Denise fixes breakfast for the family, and Alan is determined to take eight-year-old Mattie, the eldest, to school himself.

Denise was always determined to get a college education. Even after her marriage, despite the economic constraints of having been reared in a nonindustrial community, she earned a bachelor's degree in elementary education—a four-year diploma she garnered in three. She faced her first class in 1981.

She entered with all of the teaching aids that she had been taught to use while in college. She had her desk neatly arranged, complete with pull-out tissues that seem to go with grade school teachers as much as apples.

By the end of her first day, her formerly orderly room was a shambles.

"Were you discouraged after that first day?" I asked.

"I really was," she said. "In our school system in our hometown, new teachers always got the schools that had the rougher children. I hate to say children that don't really get as much attention, but it was the children that were a little more difficult. That first year was really tough. But I can look back and think about how sweet they were and so needy for my attention. I remember the little black girls who used to love to brush my long blonde hair. I'd get my brush and they'd stroke my hair. They were sweet children who needed a lot of attention."

By 1985, on the urging of a good friend, Denise quit teaching to become a flight attendant. The hours were shorter, the vacation time longer, and the salary higher.

She was required to move to Greensboro, North Carolina, for flight training for six months. During the span, Alan was alone for the first time in their five-year marriage. And he began to write songs.

"I guess he got bored or lonely," she said. "He was living on West Point Lake, working at a marina, and he just started picking up his guitar and writing songs. Those were some of the first songs he ever wrote, and they were very crude. We had a trailer on the lake, and he'd come home in the evening by himself and write songs."

One time, when Alan might have been writing a song, Denise was in the Atlanta airport en route to Greensboro. Alan had earlier said that he had decided the couple should move to Nashville to try their luck at writing commercial country songs, and at getting a recording deal.

"And I was going through the airport and saw Glen Campbell," Denise recalled. "And I thought, Man, I really hate to approach this guy but I've got to do it, you know, whether he laughs at me or whatever. I just went up to him and told him that my husband was trying to get into the music business and did he have any advice?

"And he asked me if my husband wrote songs," she continued. "I told him he did, and he gave me the business card of Marty Gamblin, who ran Glen's [music] publishing company."

Denise took the card to Alan.

In 1994, Glen Campbell published his life story, *Rhinestone Cowboy*. He remembered meeting Denise.

> "The first thing he'll [Alan] have to do is move to Nashville, Tennessee. Write to Marty Gamblin, the man who runs my music publishing companies. Have your husband send his songs to him and see what he thinks."
>
> Most songwriters I give that advice to never send anything. Those who do send songs that are mostly unusable.
>
> The woman's husband wasn't like most songwriters. He didn't write, but he called Marty. He asked him if he might drive from his Georgia home to play him some tunes.
>
> "Well, when do you want to do that?" Marty asked.
>
> "Well, I can't do it today," Marty said Alan replied.
>
> Marty agreed to meet Alan in two weeks, and at 12:30 P.M. on August 15, 1985, Alan walked into his office.

Alan and Denise could not have had a better initial Nashville contact than Marty, as he shared their family values. Marty stressed that Alan would have to move to Nashville, but urged him not to if it meant breaking up his family.

Marty told Alan that he couldn't put him on a weekly draw immediately, because Alan's talents were too "green," Marty recalled. He told Alan to find a job outside the music business somewhere in Nashville, and to call him when that happened.

Three weeks later, Marty said, his telephone rang.

"I'm here," he quoted Alan as saying. "I got a job in the mailroom at the Nashville Network. What do we do now?"

Nashville Now was then the flagship show for the Nashville Network. Alan became the mail boy for Ralph Emery, the show's host and dean of Nashville broadcasters. Alan did not tell his boss that he was seeking a record deal, fearing he would not be hired. He instead contended he had moved to Nashville to be with Denise who, he said, had been transferred here by her employer.

"I don't know," Marty said he told Alan. "Usually, when I give people my move-to-Nashville spiel, I never see them again. But we'll think of something."

Eventually he became a staff writer for Glen Campbell Music, earning an advance against royalties of one hundred dollars a week.

Denise kept flying, and Alan kept trying to get a recording contract. She'd hit the clouds and he'd pound the pavement, and Alan's career still seemed to be going nowhere fast.

She agreed to move with Alan to Nashville. After all, she said, she could be a flight attendant based out of Tennessee and commute to her home base in Washington, D.C.

She said she relied on Alan to find an apartment. She said it was a dump.

"I said, 'You know, Alan, I love you very much but I am not living here,'" she recalled. The final straw was a shooting inside a nearby building in the complex.

"It just so happened that Alan saw a note at the Nashville Network that a basement apartment was for rent," Denise recalled. "Alan approached Tim Thompson [the landlord] and we rented that place for $350 a month."

The couple lived in that basement for five years until Mattie was born in 1990. Denise, to this day, says she loved the little place. The Jacksons became friends with the landlord, who cried when they moved out.

Alan, Denise, and the baby came to my house that same year, and Mattie cried the entire time. Alan surmised it was because the infant was a stranger to natural light.

"You'd cry too if you were seeing windows for the first time," he told George and me.

Alan was turned down by every major record

label in Nashville during the five years they lived in the basement. Some labels turned him down twice.

Denise said she often came home from flights only to hear him lament that he was sure he was never going to get a record deal. The couple agreed to give Nashville five years, and Alan got his record deal on the fourth. Had he not, they would have returned to Georgia, Denise said, where Alan could have worked as a car salesman, as he had done previously, or returned to the marina.

"I look back on those times and even though they were rough financially, I think we were probably close, and had some of our most intimate times during those years," Denise said. "We didn't have people around us doing everything for us and it was just the two of us by ourselves trying to reach a goal; they were very intimate times.

"I love to tell this story," she went on. "There was a female record executive at a label at the time that listened to Alan's demos. I guess they had a meeting and she told him that he did not have star quality and she recommended that he go back to Georgia. Alan is stubborn. Don't tell him what he can't do. I guess some people would have just got discouraged and would have tucked tail and headed back home. But you know, for him it just fueled the fire. He told me he was going to show her he could make it in the business."

Neither Alan nor Denise has said "I told you so" to the executive, and she has never admitted she was wrong.

Denise took a maternity leave to have her second child and planned to return to work as a flight attendant from force of habit—the habit of helping her husband. By then, Alan's second album was approaching sales of four million units, after similar success on his first.

"'Denise,'" he said to me one day, 'I think you can quit your job now.' I was just going to hang on to that little job."

And then Denise said something that I've heard from more Nashville wives than anything. She became afraid of being forgotten by the man whose career she had helped create. I know. I asked her point-blank.

"Was there a hard time adjusting to his success?" I asked. "Did you feel he didn't need you anymore?"

"That is right on target," Denise said, without hesitation. "Let's see, he toured with Randy Travis on his first year. And he was all of a sudden getting lots and lots of media attention. I'd just had the baby in June of '90, and a lot of major things happened within six months—I had the baby, his career took off, I quit my flying job. Now I had always worked all of my life, and all of a sudden I'm home by myself with a baby, and Alan's gone all of the time on the road."

"And like most wives," I said, "you thought he was out there having a good time when you were at home."

"Right," she said, "and I went through a period of resentment because I thought, I supported you basically for the last five years financially and now you're out having a ball, a great time on the road performing for all these admiring fans and I'm at home with a colicky baby. So yes, I went through a little resentment and a little depression. But now, looking back, I can see that it was perfect timing because he didn't want me on the road with him. He was out there trying to figure out who he was and what his show was supposed to be. And that time gave me a lot of one-on-one time with the baby, and let me figure out what I was supposed to be doing as a mother."

She said she is glad that Alan's success came after they had been married for ten years. Had it come earlier, when he was less mature, she isn't sure he could have handled it—the temptation toward an inflated ego and other pressures.

Denise recalled a conversation we had years ago about how rumors always circulate about a male celebrity's unfaithfulness. I remember getting letters from women claiming they had been with George, and I warned Denise that similar things would happen to her. I was very proud of the way she handled a 1995 Nashville buzz about Alan and a female singer with whom he had toured. Some of the stories were hair-raising, and of course they were all supposedly attributed to somebody who claimed to know the truth.

"You know what, Alan and I probably didn't hear about that until probably six months after it had been circulating and you know it's silly because how could it have happened? Alan flies to every one of his shows. He gets there in time to do his meet-and-greet [a social time with fans] and walks onstage and then he flies home. So in my mind, there is no physical way he could have had anything to do with anybody else.

"But you know what?" Denise continued. "He told me, 'Denise, you look back at every artist that has ever toured with the opposite sex.'"

She said Alan acknowledged rumors that had once surrounded Kenny Rogers and Dolly Parton, Garth Brooks and Trisha Yearwood, and virtually every other male-female act in country music. He was right. I've heard them all, and so has virtually any of the other approximately 25,000 people who work in the Nashville music industry.

"Nancy," she said, "I don't have insecurities now. Alan has said to me, 'I'm too old and wise regarding other women. I'm exactly where I want to be, so why would I mess that up?'

"And I believe him," she went on. "We're obviously doing fine. And the other person [in the rumor] is happily married with a family.

"You know," Denise continued, "Alan says he would never want to get remarried because he wouldn't know if the person really wanted him."

"You mean he'd wonder if that person was simply after his money?"

"Yes," she said. "It's unfortunate, but when you get to the position we're in, you're not as trustful."

"What is the most significant change that money has made in your life?"

"Well," she said, "obviously I don't have to do

things that other people do. I mean, I don't have to clean my house. I don't have to buy groceries if I don't want to, even though that's something I still enjoy doing from time to time. And then I enjoy becoming a celebrity by association. I mean, that's something I never dreamed I would have to deal with."

"Do you like it?"

"I feel proud," she said, "when people come and say, 'You're Alan Jackson's wife.' I feel extremely proud and most of the time it's not a bother. The only time it ever kind of bothers me is when we're at a function that our children are participating in. You know, when we're at Mattie's softball game and we're trying—and Alan is trying to watch the game and people are coming up, wanting to talk when it distracts us from our children."

Denise is wise beyond her years. She is planning for her daughters' futures by not making plans. I talked about the rough times she and Alan underwent, and asked how she would feel if one of her daughters wanted to marry a musician.

"Nancy," she pondered, "you know, you can't stop your children from doing what they want to do and if any of them wanted to be in the music business I certainly wouldn't stop them. I guess I would just hope and pray that the person they married would be a decent person and would be good to them. I'd rather they marry a decent musician than some businessman that wouldn't treat them right.

"You know what I think about our family? When Alan's career is finally over, he's not going to be one of those who goes into a big depression. His ego just isn't like that.

"He really is content to sit at home with his family and enjoy his hobbies."

And his family is obviously content to have him.

"Alan and I sometimes feel guilty about all that we have because it is still so foreign to us," Denise said. "But we think about all of the families that depend on us for a paycheck and that makes us feel that this is okay. I just hope that our girls will have the values we did.

"Mattie will ask, 'Mommy, are we rich?' And I'm honest with her and I tell her that we do have a lot more than other people. Therefore, we can give more. Their little nursery school takes up toys for the hobby shop and instead of giving one toy we buy thirty toys. We can give more because we have more and that doesn't make us any more special. We have a lot—but that comes with the responsibility of giving back.

"That's my ultimate hope for them—that they will grow up and have some sense of values and be good children, that they will not be little brats.

"I don't think they will be."

"A lot has happened in my life—both personally and in my marriage since Nancy interviewed me last summer. Alan moved out of our house on December 26, 1997. We did not reconcile until May 1998 when he moved back in. Until this point in my life, I have had no major crises of any kind other than the sudden death of my brother Ron in April 1994. This separation was the most devastating experience I have ever gone through in my life. I couldn't imagine being faced with the possibility of being divorced from the only man I had ever loved—the man I had been with for twenty-two years of my life.

"I realize that most long-term marriages go through a crisis of some sort at some time—celebrities are no exception. Alan's high-profile status certainly made it even more difficult. As I write this now, I can see that this difficult time has really been a blessing for me. Our separation was a 'wake-up' call for both of us. It forced us to deal with issues that had never really been dealt with before. Our relationship is now based on mutual love and respect—not mutual neediness, as so many relationships are.

"Our four and a half months of separation also caused me to cling to the One who has always loved me unconditionally and has always wanted the best for me—my heavenly Father. This crisis brought me back to Him like nothing else could. Because of this new walk with Him, I have a 'peace that passes all understanding' as the Bible says. I know that if things had not worked out in my marriage, I would still have a joy and contentment that no houses, jewelry, boats, airplanes, or even a gorgeous celebrity husband could bring me. It was not until I totally surrendered my marriage to Him that miracles began to happen in our relationship. I can say firsthand that God *does* work in mysterious ways. To God be the glory!"

11

Not every "Nashville wife" agreed to participate in this book. Some thought their celebrity husbands' public lives provided more than enough international focus on their households. They didn't want to be in a book that put their marriage under a larger magnifying glass. I understand.

A couple of wives wanted to be paid for their stories. No one who was interviewed for this book was paid anything for any reason. I didn't want anyone to say that some of the reports were exaggerated for financial incentives.

I had one request to the wives who cooperated. I told them I knew that they wouldn't tell everything about their marriages. Their bedroom habits, for example, are nobody's business. What they chose to tell, I asked them to tell honestly.

The result, to the best of their ability, is truthful text.

It would be unfair if I didn't apply the same rules of frankness to myself that I sought from other wives. I'm going to endeavor to make my chapter the most personal part of the book. It's no secret that I've been married for fifteen years, and have been a soulmate for seventeen with a man who formerly had the reputation of being the biggest drunk, cocaine addict, domestically violent man in country music—and, some say, in all of show business. George once thought the mark of a great country singer was to bare his soul, touch your heart, and throw up in his boots. I confess all of that honestly. Just as honestly, I tell you he's a changed man. George today still has the voice of a vocal genius combined with the temperament of a lamb. He's the most generous man I've ever known. I intend to discuss some of his specific acts of kindness later in this chapter.

The nation, and especially the press, is fascinated with my husband. He's the only singer in country music who, during the 1960s to 1980s, made as many headlines for his outrageous and lawless behavior as he did for his music. And his music has made him the most critically acclaimed country singer who ever lived. The Village Voice once wrote that George Jones "should be on a list of America's top-ten best singers in any category." Penthouse called him "the Holy Ghost of country music." The published and broadcast accolades are endless.

Yet the most frequent question I've been asked about George has been, "Nancy, why did you stay?"

I have several answers, but one is overriding. I knew I could save not only his career, but his life itself. I actually believed that if I left him, the drug dealers would kill him. I somehow felt that would leave George's blood on my hands. Also, I knew the real George Jones was not the maniac I saw when he was taking drugs and alcohol. I am a determined person. I don't quit. I was determined to get him sober or die trying. Literally. Once he was sober, I knew I'd have the man I'd always wanted.

For now, I'll simply tell the story of George and me, and perhaps you'll come up with your own answer regarding our longevity. We celebrated our fifteenth wedding anniversary on March 4, 1998. Including the time we dated and lived together, we have been an item for seventeen years.

George has been drug- and drunkenness-free for twelve years. He occasionally has a glass of wine before dinner. I'm talking about a man who used to drink a quart of wine before getting out of bed by noon. He was often mean while drinking, and he made the devil look like a sissy when he combined alcohol with cocaine.

I hate illegal drugs to this day. I'll fire anyone in our organization who uses them. I fired a man last year who had done some work for George and me because I had established that he was smoking crack cocaine. Someone said what he did on his own time was his own business. Bullshit. That stuff stays in the user's system for three days. If you pitch a Saturday-night binge, you're still under the influence when you come to work on Monday. Marijuana stays in the human system for thirty days.

Don't even try to defend recreational drug use to me, and, in fact, don't call it recreational. Call it life-ruining.

During George's reckless days, he had comparatively few days of sobriety. Even back then, when sober, George was the kindest man I'd ever met. He has remained so during twelve years of sobriety. Like the fine wine he used to drink, his quality only improves with the passing of time.

Here is our story.

* * *

I was born in Coushatta, Louisiana, sixty miles south of Shreveport, to a father who was a logger and a mother who was a housewife. I was reared in Mansfield and was imbued with the work ethic at an early age.

Seventeen years ago, I was working in Shreveport on a mass-production assembly line where I built the component boards to go inside telephones. It was piecework. In other words, the more telephones I built, the more I was paid. Long before I left that job, I could assemble the parts of a telephone in about sixty seconds. My workweek was forty hours, but management allowed the option of working twenty additional hours weekly if I wanted. For those twenty hours I was paid a higher hourly and assembly rate. I always took the overtime, as I needed the money. I even worked Sundays. I eventually was a single mother with two daughters, Sherry and Adina, and needed money badly. Sherry lived with her father, and both girls were children. My weekly take-home pay was three hundred dollars.

Now this may be hard to believe, but I honestly wasn't aware of George's highly publicized criminal track record. Working sixty hours a week and trying to be a mother and homemaker, I didn't have time to absorb a lot of news. Many of his antics were reported in the tabloids, but in those days I didn't read tabloids. My world was closed and was mostly a nonstop marathon of work, motherhood, and too little rest. I didn't spend a lot of time listening to music, going to shows, or partaking in other amusements. I actually enjoyed my job, as it was a challenge. Management would say it had to have so many units by a certain day, and I enjoyed the challenge of a deadline.

About all I knew of George Jones was that he was that great country singer who had been married to Tammy Wynette.

In my workaday world, I didn't expect ever to meet him or any other famous entertainer. And I wasn't impressed with his published antics. I had a temper myself as a young person. I once drove a car through the front window of a tavern because they had cut off the service of liquor to me. I crashed through the glass and they still didn't serve me.

My girlfriend Linda Morris was at the Louisiana Downs horse racing track in Shreveport in November 1981 when she was approached by Wayne Oliver, George's former manager. Wayne wanted to date Linda. George asked Wayne to get a date for him too, and Wayne asked Linda if she knew anyone. She called and asked if I'd like to meet George Jones. I said no. She said it would be fun. I said I'd heard he was wild. She reminded me that I was a little wild. How often did I meet anyone famous? So I said yes. At least I'd get an autograph and have something to tell my friends on the assembly line.

George, Wayne, and Linda went to New York City the next day. I was asked to meet them there.

Not only was I going to meet a star, I was going to get to go to New York for the first time. They said they would pay my fare, and I agreed to go with the stipulation that George not expect me to sleep with him. Before I departed, I was assured of a separate room. I was also assured that he was not married, and he wasn't.

I entered George's New York hotel room and we began talking instantly. I wondered if all celebrities were so normal and easygoing. We talked all night, and I saw the sun rise among the Manhattan skyscrapers. I went to my room, rested, and returned to Louisiana. George continued his tour of one-night performances.

I wondered if I'd ever hear from him again, especially since I had not been the sexual pushover to which he was accustomed.

In the late 1970s and early 1980s, George reportedly missed more personal appearance engagements than he kept, and almost always blamed his absence on alcohol, drugs, or management problems. I didn't know that either. He had no reluctance to stand up an audience that had paid good money to buy tickets to see him.

Consequently, in 1982 he had no hesitation about returning to Shreveport to see me. He simply blew off the shows where he was booked to appear. Thousands of people were left in the lurch because he wanted to see one person—me. At the time, he was regularly sued by concert promoters, and usually lost by default. He didn't care about that. Why bother going to court? He felt he had no defense anyhow.

Years later, in 1995, I packed the entire trunk of a new Cadillac Sedan De Ville as well as the backseat with lawsuits that had been settled years earlier against George. I gave the papers to Tom Carter as research material for George's autobiography, *I Lived to Tell It All,* which was published in 1996. They were only half of the lawsuits that had been brought against George since I'd known him. One of George's lawyers said he thinks George lost all of them by default.

I'll tell you right now that the thing I like best about George is his unpredictability, even though it sometimes frustrates me. I mean, he's asked me to plan parties, then only briefly come out of his room when guests arrived. We bought a home in Florida in 1997 where we were supposed to spend the winter. We stayed two days, George started talking about coming home, and we were back on our Tennessee farm in less than two weeks. Imagine—we had icy roads and temperatures in the upper teens in Tennessee, while our Florida seaside villa sat warm and empty.

That's vintage George.

I guess I first experienced George's unpredictability when he called a few days after that first trip to New York City. I was working the assembly line when someone said I had a long-distance call.

George identified himself, asked how I'd been,

and asked if it was snowing in Shreveport. Just small talk. Then, just as nonchalantly, he asked me to quit my job and become his constant companion. I couldn't believe my ears. I wondered if the telephone was defective—and if I'd built it.

I was stunned, and my boss was outraged.

"Do you know who this guy is?" he asked.

"Yes," I said, "he's real nice. I spent the night with him in New York."

"You did what?"

"Well, not that way," I said. "We talked and talked until daylight."

I told him I didn't want to hear anything about what he had read about George Jones. I knew the real man, I said, and I was going to accept his invitation to run away.

I was in my early thirties.

My boss was really upset. I could tell by the way he kept patting his chest and struggling to inhale.

It was summertime, so Adina, then fourteen, traveled with George and me in a recreational vehicle. George's band traveled in a bus ahead of us.

Before I quit the phone component job others told me about George's drinking. I was sure they were exaggerating, and that if he did drink too much, I could help him taper off. Why do women always think they can change a man?

I soon saw firsthand that George had two personalities. He didn't know the meaning of moderation. He got stumbling drunk. He often drank until he passed out, woke up violently ill, and immediately ran to the whiskey to steady his nerves. Then he'd get so steady he couldn't move.

I had only begun to formulate my antidrinking plan when George pulled out the cocaine. I had never seen the drug, much less seen anyone use it.

"What is that?" I asked.

George thought I was making fun of him and responded in anger. He would do so more times. The old George Jones exhibits new behavior that is nothing like the violent man he used to be when under the influence of the drugs he no longers uses, or the whiskey he no longer drinks.

I don't believe the old behavior was directly from George Jones, but was a result of the drugs and alcohol inside him. I knew there was a wonderful person beneath those substances, and time has proven I was right. I stayed with George because I knew we'd be happy if I could get him sober. I did, and we are.

Soon after I met George, he thought he might do better regarding drug and alcohol avoidance if he could escape the show business environment. Nashville had many people who were into substance abuse as much as George was, and it also had a lot of painful memories for him. He'd been married for six years to Tammy, his third wife, and a lot of folks still mentally paired them.

So George, Adina, and I moved to Muscle Shoals/ Florence, Alabama, home of his friends Peanut and Charlene Montgomery. Peanut was a lay preacher and a nondrinker. I was willing to try anything to get George sober.

It didn't work. I felt that George's financial contributions to Peanut's nondenominational church were too generous. And it's not as if we were rich in those days.

I began voicing my opinion to George about his financial affairs and I told him what I thought about his friends the Montgomerys. George resented that, as his friendship with Peanut went back a long way. They had written many hit songs together. Peanut had forgiven George when George got fed up with Peanut's preaching. He asked Peanut to stop preaching, and Peanut kept condemning George for his drinking and drugging. So George fired a pistol into Peanut's car door on the driver's side while Peanut was behind the wheel. That had happened a few years before I met any of them.

After we'd moved to Alabama, we went to the Montgomerys' church one Sunday morning and Peanut railed from the pulpit about the evils of men and women living together while not married. He knew George and I were cohabiting. I think everybody in the congregation knew. His public comments made George angry, and we walked out of the church and out of the Montgomerys' lives.

Unbeknownst to me, George's cocaine habit was worsening. I didn't see how it could get any worse, as it was already monopolizing his life. Adina, now fifteen, was smart enough to figure out what was happening. She loved the sober George, and he loved her. But she couldn't stand what she was seeing and moved back in with her father in Shreveport. She'd get homesick for George and me, and I'd promise her he had changed because he had made that promise to me. So she'd return to Muscle Shoals/Florence, and George might be sober a few days before pulling a weeklong bender. He was putting me in a place where I had to choose between him and my daughter. I chose the husband, hoping he would love the daughter enough to make a home for her and me. Eventually, that's what happened.

The Muscle Shoals/Florence madness continued as George began to visit a recreation hall. He just sat me down on a bench, went into a back room, and emerged with a happy and hyperactive personality.

I got it. George was getting cocaine inside the joint.

I had to find a way to stop it. I told a man inside the place I was going to call the police. He advised against it. I recognized the tone in his voice. The man was more than a street dealer. He was a major supplier. I'd seen enough television to know what suppliers do to people who tell law enforcement personnel about them.

I never quit anything I start. I was going to see this thing through until George saw through the demons that were killing him. Down deep, I *knew* I could find a way to get him drug- and alcohol-free.

I made friends with a local man called Big Daddy.

He confirmed my suspicions and told me where George was getting his cocaine.

I also began to develop suspicions about George's management. One of his managers was later arrested and served time for dealing cocaine. George was a drug addict whose obedience the manager could ensure by seeing that George stayed hooked on cocaine. So the supplier was getting rich, and the manager who wanted George to be his puppet was firmly against my attempts to help George rehabilitate.

I'd leave the house to buy groceries, and return to find George missing. He'd be gone with his manager.

Hours later, the phone might ring. The caller was my informant, Big Daddy. He'd tell me where I could find George. Sure enough, I'd go to a dark and dirty place, and there would sit George. I wondered if some men in George's life and career were trying to kill him through substance abuse.

I had to find a way to prevent George from being by himself. They'd never get drugs to him if I were around, I foolishly thought. Adina was not old enough to drive legally, but I let her drive nonetheless. She went to the grocery store and did all of the household errands. The dealers would see her leave by herself and know that I was in the house with George.

One day they bolted inside—uninvited and unannounced. I began cussing and telling them to get out, but there were too many people running in too many directions. Before I knew it, George was out of my sight. By the time I got to him he was high and his money was gone. It happened numerous times.

I called the police, but eventually told the police to their faces that they were on the take from the dealers. George said the same thing, and wrote his accusations in *I Lived to Tell It All*.

After all, was I supposed to believe that in a small town like Muscle Shoals the cops couldn't get to our house before the dealers got out? I didn't know the dealers' names, and many times different men showed up. I was a prisoner in my own home. The dealers were walking in and out at will.

I remember one guy knocked once and said he had brought a guitar as a gift for the great George Jones. I was suspicious. I removed the guitar and opened the compartment for picks and capos. It was full of cocaine.

George was steadily losing his mind to whiskey and cocaine. They could get to him at home and, on the road, through his management. All George had to do was see alcohol or cocaine and he was a goner. They had made him that way. I meant what I said about losing his mind.

He forgot he was George Jones and developed two alternate personalities. One belonged to an old man, the other to a duck. He would go for days without speaking. He would simply quack his way through slurred English. Then the voice of the old man would emerge and tell him to stop talking so foolishly. Then the two personalities would clash, and a violent argument would ensue.

Sometimes I shook George and told him to snap out of it. Sometimes he didn't even hear me.

I was at my mental and emotional end. Spent. I was ready to leave the man I so desperately wanted to help. Eventually, I would pack my clothes and daughter and drive away, only to return, knowing I was leaving him at the mercy of men who were letting him kill himself.

From out of the blue, Big Daddy called and confirmed my suspicions. My caretaking of George was unappreciated. His "caretakers" wanted me out of the way.

Big Daddy again warned me that I was in over my head. He advised that I take George far away from the crooked and virtually lawless deep and semirural south. An honest law enforcement officer there couldn't live on his salary, Big Daddy said, so there weren't any honest lawmen, he insisted.

As it turned out, Big Daddy was right. One day, I was driving across a bridge over a river between Muscle Shoals and Florence. My car was repeatedly rammed from behind. Adina was screaming and so was I.

The car jolted to the railing, and Adina and I braced for the long fall to the black water below. Instead, I turned into oncoming traffic. There was no shoulder on either side of the road. I drove in the wrong lane until an approaching car forced me back into my own. Then I was rammed again, and again I veered intentionally into the wrong lane to avoid plunging into the water.

The driver who was pummeling me from behind knew he would either force me into a head-on collision or into the river. I made it across the bridge and knew my daughter and I had been the victims of attempted murder.

It got worse.

The telephone rang and a voice I recognized as belonging to one of the thugs who had delivered cocaine to my helpless companion said he wanted to come to my house. I told him to go to hell. That was the most polite thing I said.

"But what about Adina?" the man asked.

"What do you mean?" I asked.

"We have her," he said.

Click.

I completely lost it. I was hysterical beyond description. Incredibly, George was straight. He had not had a drink or drugs for a few days. He struggled to comfort me, but I wouldn't have it. I physically fought him as he tried to restrain me. He was shouting at me. I saw his lips move and the veins protrude in his neck. But I couldn't hear a thing.

The thugs had my first-born daughter.

My screaming was interrupted by the telephone ringing again. I watched it, fearful to answer. The caller was Big Daddy.

I had my heart in my mouth and a gun in my purse when I stormed into Big Daddy's nightclub. He indicated that I should subtly look under the bar. I did, and there, on a shelf, lay my fifteen-year-old daughter, curled up and eating popcorn.

Big Daddy never told me how he had gotten her. He only told me to get home quickly. I didn't arrive quickly enough. The thugs had run into my house as soon as I'd gone after Adina.

I had been through financial deprivation, an attack on my life, the kidnapping of my child, and life with a violent drunk and drug addict.

And I stayed, although George and I weren't even married.

I knew we had to get out of the Muscle Shoals/ Florence area but didn't see how we could while we were constantly being watched. Nonetheless, we tried. I loaded my car with George's and my stuff and put additional things in a car driven by Adina, still too young to drive legally. To make a long story short, I stopped at a red light, went forward when the light turned green, and was arrested.

The night became alive with swirling red lights. A cop jerked me out of the car and put me in handcuffs.

"What's this about?" I demanded.

"You ran that red light," he said.

I called him a liar, and said he was on the take from hoodlums.

He took George and me to jail. Adina, meanwhile, had driven back to the house we had tried to flee in the dark.

I was cussing every cop in the station as George kept telling me to be quiet.

I told him he was a fool, that the cops were going

to put me in jail, take him away, and let the goons load him up on cocaine. I said it was another dance with his crooked associates to get him to do what they wanted. And what they wanted was for him to agree to work shows for little or no money.

I was right.

Uniformed officers locked me in a cell and took George from the police station. I spat through the bars at the cops and called them foul names I wouldn't use here.

George was back within thirty minutes. He had signed contracts agreeing to do shows that paid little or nothing, and he was high. Without explanation, a policeman opened my cell door and smiled as he told me I could go.

I kicked him repeatedly in the shins, and for good reason. I couldn't kick high enough to clobber his nuts.

I was never arrested, only detained, and the thugs had won again. It would be another week with little or no income. They always got the money.

George and I, defeated, drove to the house we had tried to escape. Adina sat inside a locked car in the driveway, sobbing. She too thought that I had gotten us into a life from which there was no escape.

So George decided to go underground. That meant quitting show business. He said he'd do anything to keep the three of us together, and that he couldn't do that if people could find us. So, by dark of night, we moved to Louisiana, not sure what we would do for a living.

We were broke.

But we were safe and together in a modest place in Lafayette, Louisiana.

We could barely afford a telephone. One night it rang and someone said they knew Big Daddy had been helping George and me. I denied everything. I said the caller should talk to Big Daddy. He said Big Daddy couldn't talk, as his head had been detached from his body. I never told anyone his real name, although many people in a small place like Muscle Shoals know who he was.

To this day, his death by decapitation remains unsolved.

George has done irreparable damage to his central nervous system. He still cannot take the slightest emotional pressure. I realized in 1982 that if I was going to stay with this man I was going to have to learn to manage his career. If it became pressurized, which is the nature of show business, George would simply walk away.

He published his life story in 1996 and was visited by a crew from *60 Minutes* about the book. George was tired from a show he'd given the previous night. He simply wouldn't come out of the house while *60 Minutes* waited for him. The crew finally left, presumably to go back to New York City.

Do you realize how many books he would have sold, and how much money he would have made, had he appeared on *60 Minutes*? He didn't care, even though he had an appointment with the production crew.

So by 1982 I had learned all about booking agents, management, advances against royalties on record deals, and all that goes with running a celebrity singer's career.

George was staying relatively straight, I was becoming his manager of record, and we were having the semblance of a normal life.

Weeks after our "escape" from Muscle Shoals/Florence, however, George's old drug-dealing managers showed up wanting to visit with him in private.

I begged him not to go with them. He did, and I didn't hear from him for two weeks. I listened to the news on the hour and half hour for fourteen days, knowing that I'd hear if a dead body had been identified as his.

Then George called. He said he was coming home, and that he wanted to get professional help. He wanted to go to a hospital.

He arrived dirty and out of his mind, babbling in the voices of the old man and the duck. But George, Adina, and I set out for a rehabilitation center. We stopped at a motel, and Adina went to her room. George and I went to ours.

I should have known something was wrong when he called me by the wrong name—a man's name. Then he called me another man's name. I recognized the names as the men back in Muscle Shoals/Florence who had held George prisoner.

"George, what is wrong with you?" I said. "I'm Nancy."

He exploded at me for falsifying my identity, and then he became physically aggressive. My wounds healed.

George and I were broke when he eventually decided he wanted to move to Texas, his home state. He thought that walking the soil of his youth in the thick woods of East Texas would be perfect therapy as well as an escape from the trappings of the city and show business.

And so I followed.

We lived in a mobile home. At times in his life, George had lived in lavish mansions. Land was cheap in rural East Texas, and soon we acquired enough to open an outdoor concert hall.

Actually, it was little more than benches and a covered stage.

We called it Jones Country. Suddenly, George Jones didn't have to go on the road to perform for his fans. His fans could come to him. And they did, for a while, in cars and recreational vehicles.

I cooked at that place. I cleaned toilets. I did anything to help the latest attempt at a real life by my man. And he was my man.

One day, as I was on my hands and knees in the garden, he walked up to me and simply said, "If you're going to be the next Mrs. Jones you'd better get up from there and let's go get a blood test."

Pretty romantic, eh?

We had twenty dollars and a sack of beans. That was our entire net worth when we were married by a preacher in the home of Helen Scroggins, George's sister. There is an Instamatic wedding picture.

Helen cut a wedding cake, and George told her we had no time to eat. We had a park to build, he said.

It was March 4, 1983.

George and I drove twenty miles to Jasper, Texas, and had our wedding dinner at Burger King.

Later that year, he started grinding out hit songs. It appeared a comeback was under way.

But I'm overlooking one more story in the George and Nancy saga.

Because I was not George's wife in 1982, I had no legal authority to have him committed to a drug and alcohol center for the second time. He wanted to go and asked his sister to sign the papers.

As we drove toward the rehab center, Adina and I began to beg George for the thousandth time not to use cocaine. We began to challenge him to throw it out the car window. Our challenge became a chant.

He took a mighty snort, and while riding its courage, threw his dope out the window. Adina and I cheered.

In no time, George regretted his decision and wanted back the cocaine lost in weeds miles behind us. He became furious. He leapt over the front seat and put his foot on top of mine, which was on the accelerator. He did that simply because he was very impaired.

Our speed increased dramatically. We were going ninety-one miles per hour when the cop stopped us.

I was arrested for speeding, reckless driving, and related charges.

Then the cop recognized George. He got on his radio and called the Bureau for Narcotics and told them to bring a drug dog.

I asked why, and he looked at me blankly.

That's George Jones, he said, there's got to be drugs around somewhere.

And there were.

When George threw his drugs out the window, some had blown back into the backseat. The dog smelled it, and George was arrested for possession of cocaine and public drunkenness.

I wasted my breath trying to tell the authorities that we were en route to a drug treatment center.

George was put in handcuffs. Adina broke into tears. I had a little dog that began barking at the big drug dog. There were so many cops it looked like a policeman's convention.

George was placed in one cell, Adina and I in another.

The sheriff, an honest man, walked into the room. We were near Jackson, Mississippi.

"Who the hell put this woman and this kid and this dog in this cell?" he said. I had been yelling and screaming. This time it worked. They let Adina and me go. Soon they opened George's cell too.

I actually think they set us free just to get me to shut up. George thinks so too.

The next day's newspaper had a headline that said "George Jones Charged with Cocaine Possession." An accompanying story said George was "a loser beyond help." It called him a "Godless immoral pauper."

Now get this: He wanted to sue the newspaper for libel!

He demanded that his lawyer accuse that newspaper of defaming him and damaging his good name. The lawyer insisted that George had no chance of winning.

No horror movie was ever more outrageous than my courtship with George Jones.

George passed out shortly after we were released from jail. He awakened in the backseat of the car with a terrible hangover. He decided he didn't want treatment after all.

Adina and I pleaded, and he physically pushed us out of the car. We watched his taillights speed into the distance.

Adina and I walked to a farmhouse and I told the woman who answered the door that I had been ejected from a car driven by George Jones. There we were, disheveled, lost, and claiming to have been kicked out of a vehicle by country's living legend.

That old farm woman didn't bat an eye.

"I can believe that," she said.

"You can?" I said.

"Yep," she said. "I got a police scanner and he's just had a wreck about two miles from here."

George was loaded into an ambulance from

which there was no escape. He was placed in a detoxification center in Birmingham, Alabama, and Adina and I went to see him regularly during his entire stay.

He was supposed to stay for days, but he was expelled, as he tested positive for drugs he had scored inside the hospital in only a couple of days.

I took a lot of classes and watched a lot of training films about how to live with an alcoholic and drug addict. I don't know why, one day in 1982, George walked into our house, took one hit of cocaine, and threw the rest down the sink. He hasn't touched the stuff ever since.

George's drinking got even worse, and he would pass out to the point of being totally unconscious. A couple of times I truly thought he had drunk himself to death.

His longtime friend and bus driver, Pee-Wee Johnson, our financial manager, Debbie Doebler, and I tricked him. He thought he was going with us to see my mother, when in fact we were taking him back to Birmingham. I had tried other rehabilitation centers closer to Nashville (we had moved there by then), but none would take George.

Too many doctors told me too many times that he was simply incurable.

Hospital attendants left the whiskey bottle in George's hand as they hoisted him from the car into the wheelchair. He was given an injection and awakened two days later.

I've talked more in this chapter about my courtship with George Jones than I have my marriage. The marriage, by comparison, is boring. It's so wonderfully boring.

Of course, there have been a few icebreakers.

Tom T. Hall and his wife, Dixie, hired a stripper for George's birthday party. I think it was his sixty-second. We were living in Brentwood and this gal began to dance around, slowly taking off her clothes.

Believe it or not, George is a modest person. He doesn't like to see people in states of undress, including family members. I could see the embarrassment and anger swelling in his face. I think I gave the stripper some indication that we'd had enough of her show. But nothing would do her. She kept undressing, and I believed she was going to get naked. I feared what George might do, so I did something first.

I shoved her into our swimming pool.

I know she was trying to be erotic, but there is nothing sexy about a nearly nude woman lying on the bottom of a pool while her wig floats on the surface.

She threatened to sue me, claiming that I had ruined her heirloom watch. I paid a lot of money to replace it, then found out it was a Timex. She went on with threats of a lawsuit, claiming I had hurt her physically.

Dixie Hall called the gal and told her to drop legal proceedings or else she'd never be hired to drop her clothes ever again in Nashville.

I haven't heard from the woman since.

George only works about fifty shows a year these days. He makes every one of them—totally sober. He performs for an hour and ten minutes, and critics say he's singing better than ever.

While he's been sober we have built a two-story, fifteen thousand-square-foot farmhouse and have built additional houses on our 150 acres for our children. There is the Florida home and a dozen vehicles. We owe no one a dime and have sound investments.

George today lives only a few yards from his daughter, Susan Smith, and her children, one of whom was graduated from high school in 1998. Susan's other child was married the same month. My daughters, Adina and Sherry, also live on our estate with their husbands and children. George and I are delighted to be called Grandma and Grandpa.

I, with legendary lawyer Joel Katz, have negotiated several of George's recording contracts with MCA Records, the label for Reba McEntire and George Strait, among others. George's concerts are drawing people in droves, despite the fact that radio refuses to play his records, as is the case with most of the senior artists. In March 1998, Johnny Cash paid eight thousand dollars for a full-page advertisement in *Billboard* magazine, the music business trade publication. It showed John extending his middle finger to American radio because it would not play the songs of veteran country stars.

George and I were not about to be outdone. As of this writing, in May 1998, I have tentative plans to hire someone to photograph the enormous testicles of a Brahman bull.

I might buy a full-page advertisement in *Billboard* showing the bull's balls if radio doesn't play George's newest recording, "Wild Irish Rose." The caption will read: "If radio had any they would play George Jones." I have already printed T-shirts with basketballs, baseballs, tennis balls, and others. "If radio had any they would play George Jones," say the shirts.

"Wild Irish Rose" was also adapted into a video about a homeless person who is a Vietnam veteran. Did you know that 40 percent of America's homeless are veterans? The music video for "Wild Irish Rose" lists the number where veterans can get assistance. It's 888–777–4443. George was planning a concert, as of this writing, whose proceeds will benefit veterans. He's selling T-shirts whose proceeds go to the center. If radio doesn't like George Jones, it should play his new song just to help the veterans. If radio doesn't play it, I'll probably run the *Billboard* advertisement with the bull's testicles. I still haven't decided for sure.

I continue to manage the career of the greatest country singer of all time and, for the last fifteen years, the greatest husband of all time.

People have asked if I'd go through it again.

No.

I was younger then. I could take more pain, I had more spirit. I also would not put my daughters through the agony that my courtship and early marriage to George allowed.

People can't understand how Adina and I forgave George for his treatment of us. The answer is simple. As I said earlier, that mean behavior came from the drugs and alcohol and not from the man. If George had ever treated us that way while sober, we would have left, we would have never returned, and we would have never forgiven him.

People who visit our home today who hear outrageous stories like those above think I'm exaggerating. The most aggressive behavior George currently exhibits is when he taps the dog with a rolled newspaper.

But as the old saying goes, "I wouldn't take a million dollars for the experience, I wouldn't give a nickel to do it again."

On April 5, 1998, George participated in the third birthday party for his grandson, Cameron. Our barn was filled with preschoolers and their mothers. In the middle, as if he were Santa Claus out of season, sat George. He's as mellow now as he once was rowdy.

Our employees spent the next day cleaning up after the youngsters. George and I settled in for another quiet evening at home. The telephone rang.

The caller, who mysteriously had gotten my unlisted number, said she was a reporter for the Associated Press. She wanted George to comment on the death of Tammy Wynette.

I was astonished. I told the reporter I knew nothing about it.

I called Tammy's house and talked to her sister-in-law, who confirmed the horrible news. Tammy had died in her sleep. A doctor said death had come from a blood clot in her lung.

The press became relentless, wanting comments from George about Tammy and their marriage that ended twenty-four years earlier. George and Tammy had recorded a reunion album, and had toured together in 1996. He had gone to her bedside when she was in critical condition with one of many illnesses later that year. They had become friends, and George was shaken by her passing. The tabloids, of course, implied that George was virtually paralyzed by grief. That wasn't true. How could it have been? He was busy helping to plan the funeral, and was active in comforting the immediate survivors. He went almost immediately to Tammy's house where he was needed, and did not drive around aimlessly as was reported. He thought about others during the crisis, not about an unrealistic sense of loss. He even issued a press release to make his feelings clear.

"I'm just very glad that we were able to work together and tour together again," he said. "It was very important for us to close the chapter on everything that we have been through. I know Tammy felt the same way. Life is too short. In the end we were very close friends and now I have lost that friend. I couldn't be sadder."

The press wanted something from me too.

"It was important to me to mend the relationship George had with Tammy and we did that," I wrote. "It also gave me the chance to get to know Tammy. Once I did, I truly loved her. She became my friend too. I will miss her terribly. Nashville has lost another legend and we don't have that many left."

I meant every word.

I never imagined that I'd be asked to help plan the funeral of George's ex-wife, but that's exactly what happened. George and I worked with George Richie, Tammy's husband, toward a private funeral, and a memorial service that was open to the public.

That was typical of the man some call the new George Jones. He isn't new to me, as I've lived with his reformation for more than a decade. But reputations are easy to establish, and almost impossible to live down. Some folks will always think that George Jones is a drunk and drug user. Those folks are stupid.

George makes all of his personal appearances. His television show, *The George Jones Show,* is the highest-rated show in its time slot on The Nashville Network. George is the star, and each week he has a guest who is a seasoned star, as well as a newcomer who sings genuine country music. He has no one on the program who screams or jumps up and down.

The Nashville Network wants George to do a second season's worth of shows in 1999, and at this point, I think he will.

George helps the less fortunate in ways for which he does not seek publicity. He is a devoted husband and grandfather.

George and the press have given a lot of the credit to me. I appreciate that, but mostly I have given George unconditional love in an uncommon way. I stayed when no one else would have stayed.

George and I are glad I did. We will be for as long as we both shall live.

12

I've known Mrs. Johnny (Sharon) PayCheck for about as long as I've known George Jones, whom I met in 1981. Sharon's husband, Johnny, used to play in George's band, and was one of George's old cronies. After Johnny left George's organization, I used to hate to see Johnny come around, as he and George would always get drunk, and often drug-crazed. I've had a lot of admiration for Sharon. She stayed home and raised her son when she had no idea of the whereabouts of her drunken husband. She said her son turned out to be a straight-A student whom she calls a "perfect child." I, on the other hand, used to chase my husband all over the nation during his rages, trying to save his life. I'm lucky my two daughters turned out so well and became happily married mothers.

I also respect Sharon for winning her fight against cancer, although she doesn't like to talk about it, so I didn't press the subject during the following pages. A lot of people might criticize her for standing by her man when he literally couldn't stand up. But Johnny PayCheck has been drug- and alcohol-free for ten years. I have to believe that her belief in him, when no one else believed he could recover, has much to do with his sobriety. She said the thought of Johnny taking a drink or using drugs never even crosses her mind nowadays. Johnny today is a regular speaker at Alcoholics Anonymous meetings. He helps others because Sharon helped him. As of April 1998, she had decided to return to the road with him as a traveling companion to a man in failing health. It marked her first time to travel with him in twelve years.

Almost anyone who's over age fifty can tell you where he was and what he was doing when he heard that President John Kennedy had been murdered. Almost anyone over age thirty-five can tell you the same about his recollections of the death of Elvis Presley. Sharon PayCheck can tell you where she was and what she was doing in 1985 when a friend called and asked if she'd heard about her husband.

Johnny had been absent for weeks, as was often the case during his drug and alcohol days, or should I say daze? Sharon's friend's husband got on the line and told Sharon he had heard where Johnny could be found.

"We were living in Atlanta," she remembered, "and it was in the morning. It was before Christmas and I got a call from my girlfriend, and she said, 'Have you heard about Johnny?' And she said, 'I'm going to call my husband and have him call you back and tell you what he heard.'

"I said, 'Okay.' "

Sharon suspected nothing significant.

"So her husband called me a couple of minutes

later and he said, 'Well, I heard on the radio that Johnny got into a scuffle and shot somebody up in Ohio.' He told me where he was in jail and I thought, That's where he was born.'"

Sharon doesn't recall today what she thought next because she momentarily went blank.

She had known Johnny intimately and had never known him to be violent. Now a nation filled with people who didn't know him at all knew he had shot a man—an old high-school friend—during a dispute in a bar in Johnny's home state.

Reports were sketchy. Sharon was sure of nothing except her uncertainty. She eventually learned that the man who, as of this writing, has been her husband for twenty-six years was inside a Hillsboro, Ohio, tavern, where he ran into chum Larry Wise.

Wise, still wearing a head bandage from his wound, would later testify that he was talking to Johnny about deer and turtle meat.

"Do you see me as some sort of country hick?" the singer had said, according to court testimony.

Wise said he asked Johnny if he were "looped," and that Johnny produced a gun and fired. Wise was grazed. Had the trajectory been an inch lower, Wise would have likely been killed.

Eight years earlier, Johnny had recorded "Take This Job and Shove It," a tune that became the anthem of discontented working men nationwide. It shot to number one.

The song had been released at about the same time of year as the shooting. Sharon was glued to the radio, listening to updates, and learned that her missing husband could face up to fifteen years in prison if convicted on charges stemming from the shooting.

"And you had no idea where he had been?" she was asked. "It was just before Christmas and he was just rambling around?"

She said that was true, and confirmed that weeks often passed without her hearing from him.

The plot thickened.

Johnny was indicted not only on an aggravated assault charge, but also for carrying a concealed weapon and tampering with evidence. He allegedly disposed of the handgun, which was not recovered.

Before a judge, Johnny argued that he could not spend fifteen years in prison because his wife might die from her cancer while he was inside.

Johnny, after exhausting all of his appeals, was nonetheless sentenced in 1988 to nine and one-half years in an Ohio penitentiary. The first night he was in prison, he laid down his cigarettes, alcohol, and drugs. He has not picked them up since.

His sentence was commuted two years later by Ohio Governor Richard Celeste, less than a week before the governor left office.

And through it all, Sharon waited.

She had earlier considered divorcing PayCheck. She had had enough of his absentee marriage and fatherhood.

She dated another man between the shooting and the sentencing. She even took him to dinner and invited Johnny. I wonder if Johnny squirmed a lot, and if he finished his meal. She also took him to one of Johnny's shows.

"I had my own life," she said. "It was just a matter of going down and getting a divorce. My main thing was my son. And then, when Johnny got into all this trouble, well, I thought, I felt so sorry for him, I mean, he was so pathetic."

She said Johnny called every day to ask her to help him get out of prison. And each day she took his call, and each day she tried to help.

"While you're in there," she told him, "why don't you pick up a book and read? Why don't you do something for yourself? You're not doing anything to improve yourself."

She indicated that he was spending too much energy on trying to get out, and not enough on self-improvement.

Johnny, at her insistence, eventually passed his General Education Development tests.

Sharon attended none of Johnny's hearings. She didn't even follow the proceedings in the mass media.

"I could have cared less," she said.

After Johnny's appeals were exhausted, after his imprisonment was unavoidable, she went to see him three times in two years, and returned the day he got out of prison. She and Johnny had dinner with the Ohio state representative who had crusaded for the singer's early release.

The hardest time of their lives was behind them, but the confinement had not been the only stone in the rocky road that was their relationship.

• • •

Sharon was reflective as she sat in a hotel where she was taking a break from Johnny's hospital bedside in January 1998. Johnny had begun the year with a giant New Year's Eve show starring Tim McGraw and Jeff Foxworthy in Nashville. He subsequently went on a performance tour, but was felled by asthma in the Southwest. He was flown back to Nashville, where the Baptist Hospital has a nationally recognized respiratory center.

He was taking medication that made him retain water, and had gained a lot of weight. When I'd seen him a few weeks earlier, his color was bad.

Sharon returned to Johnny's bedside minutes after talking to Tom. She and I visited two weeks later about her life and marriage.

She talked about her childhood and youth in Southern California, where she loved ice skating, surfing, Girl Scouts, and playing the steel guitar and cello. But she didn't talk much about any of that. She mostly talked about herself as she related to her husband, as did most of the Nashville wives.

She was always self-sufficient in a curious way. I mean, here's a woman who's been with the same husband for more than a quarter of a century, yet she determined she was not going to waste her life pining over his absenteeism. She didn't divorce him. She just kind of ignored him for a couple of decades.

They didn't have their first date until she was twenty-six.

PayCheck is now his legal last name, but then it

was only a stage name. His previous name was Donnie Young. He was using his stage name when Sharon met him.

"I didn't like him," she said. "I liked his singing, I didn't like him. I just didn't care for his attitude. Later on, I told him he looked like a weasel. That was my impression. I just thought he was arrogant."

She had gone with friends to see Johnny perform in Las Vegas. She later ran into him frequently at jam sessions around Southern California.

She always loved country music. In the early 1960s, country musicians used to get together to play simply for playing's sake. Today, many don't get together unless their managers approve, and then they rarely make music. Many instead argue about who gets top billing on a show, or why the performer before them got to be onstage longer than they did.

The country music business has lost its innocence. And much of its fun.

Soon she met Johnny; he asked her for a date.

"I said no," she recalled. "I'll go to a jam session with you and see you perform, you do this and that, you know, but I said I didn't want to get involved with him."

Johnny persisted, and Sharon finally agreed to a date. Perhaps she just wanted to silence his begging.

He told her that he was divorced, and she placed faith in that. Then she placed a call to his wife.

"I asked his wife if they were broken up and she said yes," Sharon said.

Later, she determined the couple was merely

irreconcilably separated, and that divorce was imminent. She told the wife that under the circumstances, she would go out with Johnny, and the wife wished her good luck.

"Did she give him a good recommendation?" Sharon was asked.

"No, nope," Sharon said, "but it didn't surprise me. She said, 'I'm finished with him.'"

She wished Sharon luck. Sharon would need it.

They went to a jam session and to see *Butch Cassidy and the Sundance Kid* on their first date.

Johnny, she said, almost instantly wanted to get married. He was as persistent toward marriage as he had been toward dating.

"So I finally said, 'If you would straighten up and give up your drugs and drinking, I'd marry you.' But I never in my wildest dreams thought he would. I'd never seen him straight."

But Johnny got sober. And Sharon kept her end of the bargain.

In 1971 he recorded "She's All I Got," and the song bolted to the top of the charts. Johnny had sobriety, a new wife, and the number-one country song in the nation.

The next year, "Someone to Give My Love To" rose to number four.

The picture would have been perfect with the presence of a child. The baby was born about the time of the nation's bicentennial. They named him Jonathon Bojangles, and thereafter called him Bo.

Sharon never gave a thought to what else in life

she and Johnny might need. But Johnny did, and he thought the need was drugs and alcohol. He returned to his old habits. It broke her heart, and would have broken her spirit, had a counselor not eventually taught her not to let it.

"Johnny—you couldn't depend on him," she said. "When he would leave, you never knew when he would be back. He was always messed up. I mean, it was ridiculous.

"Eventually he got into cocaine," she continued. "I had never dealt with anybody—didn't know anybody like that."

Sharon was not working when she met and married Johnny. She had come from an economically and emotionally solid background.

"Did you ever think about leaving?"

"Well, one year I was going to," she said. "But I didn't. I'll tell you how I managed to stay with him. We moved to Florida on the beach in Destin and I had—Bo was three, and I just decided I would have a life with Bo, and if Johnny stayed away, fine. I had to change. I had to change my attitude and I just stopped caring. I just wasn't going to let it ruin my life. I loved our son and I knew Johnny was a mess but I couldn't help him."

"Did you ever urge him to get professional help?" I asked.

"Sure, sure," she said. "I took him to a psychiatrist and he said, 'Well, I don't want Johnny to waste my time because he's not serious about changing,' and he wasn't. This went on for several years."

"But you stayed for twenty-six years?" I pressed.

"Yeah," she said. "I wouldn't really call it living with him because he was off doing his thing all the time. He was either on tour or he was messed up somewhere else. I would see him now and then. He would come home and straighten up for a couple of days."

It seemed to me as if she had wasted much of her life. Sharon disagreed, and said she pressed forward with her and her son's lives. It's Johnny, she said, who wasted a life. She said that to this day she pities him for all of the life he missed because he was "out of it" on drugs and alcohol.

He wasted days he can never recover, she said.

"I mean, I came from Hollywood," she said, "and everybody I knew there partied, but I'll tell you the thing that was different with Johnny. People in Hollywood would party maybe all weekend, but come Monday they went back to work. The party didn't continue for days, you know?"

She recalled going with her parents to see Johnny perform in Las Vegas in the 1970s, when his career was hot.

"I remember, we went into a restaurant and the maître d' came up—this gives you an idea of how bad he was—the maître d' came up and said to Johnny, 'Did you enjoy the birthday party that we gave you last month?' Johnny said, 'Oh, it was great.' The maître d' said, 'I've got a picture I want to show you.'"

"So Johnny turns to me and says he didn't know what this man was talking about and that he had never been in that restaurant before. When the maître d' came back he had a big picture of Johnny. He was passed out face forward in the birthday cake.

"They'd had a big party for him in this restaurant and he didn't remember and it was just a month earlier."

Sharon was asked if the picture made Johnny angry, but she didn't know the answer. She said she was so incredibly disgusted with him that she left Las Vegas and returned to Florida, then to their home. She became ill, was hospitalized for eight days, Johnny was nowhere to be found, and she miscarried what would have been their second child.

While Johnny was in prison, Sharon once again intensified her involvement with her son.

"I bought Bo a clarinet and then I sent him to camp and all the activities at camp in the summertime, and we lived on a lake and I fished with him every day," she said.

Eventually, there was no income, since Sharon had opted to concentrate on Bo, not on a job. So she borrowed from family and friends. When Johnny was released from prison, the couple set about the task of repaying thousands of dollars.

Sharon was asked if she suspected Johnny of being with other women when he was on his month-long drug and alcohol sprees. She acted as if the question was unnecessary.

"Probably, you know," she answered. "I just said, well, that's the way [it is]. I've made a mistake but now if I had not had a son, I would have left immediately."

I wondered about the value to the boy of Sharon's staying in a marriage where the father was absent and reckless. I wondered what perception of marriage the child must have had as he grew up.

"Johnny was straight for many years in the early part of your marriage," I noted. "Was there any particular incident that prompted his relapse?"

She said she thinks a part of Johnny's errant behavior had to do with role models. Willie Nelson, who had begun his career performing in suits and neckties, was the hottest ticket in country music in the middle 1970s. He had grown long hair and a beard, and Sharon thinks Johnny tried to emulate him.

"But Johnny didn't leave it on the stage as an act," she said.

"You're obviously a determined person," I said. "It would seem to me that you would have had many hours of frustration and brokenheartedness."

"I did," she said, "when he went back to drinking. I just couldn't understand it."

"Did you see a psychologist?"

"Oh, sure," she said. "I just thought, I can't take it, what am I going to do? I remember [the doctor] told me, 'You can't come in here and say that Johnny makes you do this or Johnny makes you do that. He only does what you allow him to do.' And I said, 'Well, then, that's it, I won't allow him to put me in [those circumstances].'"

And so her involvement with her son intensified even more.

She recalled sending Bo to a religious retreat, and

he returned to talk publicly about getting in touch with God and about how much his mother meant to him. She became emotional at the recollection.

"Were there times when you went to his school events or other events and you wished that your husband were around to go with you?"

"Yeah," she said. "That bothered me because it bothered Bo. And there were times when Johnny could have been there and he wasn't. He went to a few things, you know? I think there could have been a bigger effort on his part and there were many things . . . I raised Bo and Johnny missed out. He doesn't have the memories I have with our son."

"Were there ever times when you watched Johnny on television and thought you were viewing a stranger on the screen?"

"I'll tell you what," she said, "I didn't like to watch him. So I didn't watch any country music. I didn't listen to it anymore. I lived a good portion of my life, didn't even know what country music was. I said, There is more to life than country music."

Sharon did not attend her husband's big New Year's Eve show in Nashville last year. She saw him perform in Biloxi, Mississippi, in 1997. She said she went to that show just to see his band. Other than that, she can't remember the last time she saw him perform.

Years ago, she tried to tour with Johnny. She had her own bus where she could get away from him when he got too wild. She lasted for a year, and quit the road.

Sharon said, more than once, that Johnny has always had a big heart. It showed itself back when he was rarely sober, and it regularly manifests itself today.

She said Johnny was there for her when her dad died, and that today he does things with her that she knows he cares nothing about—such as attending ballets and museums.

"If you had your life to live again, would you marry an entertainer?"

"No, no, no," she said. "I just wouldn't do it again. I wouldn't go through it again."

13

I met Mrs. Charley (Rozene) Pride backstage at an awards show in 1983. George and Charley started telling stories about their wild days, and Rozene and I fell out laughing. Neither George nor Charley drinks today, but each has written an autobiography about the way he used to swig the booze. I remember one story Charley told about passing out and waking up the next morning with "KKK" hand-printed on the side of his car. He thought the Ku Klux Klan had visited him during the night, and then George confessed to the graffiti. I think Charley was too relieved to be angry.

I've seen Rozene at awards shows, and I love to laugh with her at what the performers are wearing. The only reason show business wives go to those affairs is to see how badly other women dress and to see who is with her husband and who is with someone else's.

I can still remember George advising me to get to know Rozene, saying she was a solid person, and that I'd like her a lot. He was right.

* * *

Rozene Pride is sitting in her lavish Dallas living room. The year is 1982, and a man in a white robe carrying a staff is walking aimlessly through her house. He's preaching from the Old Testament and perhaps dwelling on the forthcoming appearance of the Messiah. He's delirious, and according to one account, even tries to part an imaginary Red Sea. That's what Moses did.

But this man isn't a resurrected Moses. This is Charley Pride, who at that time was arguably the hottest male country singer in America. That year, he recorded two number-one records and one number-two record. He had recorded eighteen number-one songs during the previous ten years. That night he wasn't singing. He was just preaching the gospel of a pretend prophet with bare feet on pile carpeting.

He is manic-depressive and suffers "spells." During those times, small noises infuriate him and he throws televisions and VCRs out the door. Rozene watches through cautious eyes and eventually hires orderlies and nurses.

Rozene used to try to persuade Pride to lie down. When at last he did, she would tie a belt from her wrists to his waist so she would know if he tried to slip from the bed into the rest of the house, and back into his altered state of mind. Her struggle, and her exhaustion, went on for days. It was not the first or last time that she was physically and figuratively by the side of a man who was diagnosed with a mental illness.

In 1968, she was with Pride on a USO tour of

Army posts in Germany. He became uncontrollably despondent and mistakenly attributed his mood to exhaustion and the harassment he was getting from black soldiers for singing the white man's music— country music. Pride thought he would be healed by sleeping. But insomnia is a symptom of manic-depression, and sleep would not visit him. Pride was doing two shows a day, and the promoter insisted he continue his grueling schedule. Rozene, in an effort to save the mental health and possibly even the life of her man, would not allow it. She went through a series of people to demand that Pride be taken to a hospital.

In his autobiography, *Pride: The Charley Pride Story,* written with Jim Henderson in 1994, Pride wrote, "In a few hours, I was in a hospital under the constant watch of a doctor or nurse or orderly." He once tried to bolt from the room, but was restrained by nylon ropes across his chest and Rozene at his side.

Once when she was taking a rest, Pride broke from a group of patients en route to the cafeteria. He was chased by orderlies from the hospital and considered trying to escape through a manhole. He was captured and spent the next week under the constant and watchful eyes of Rozene or an orderly.

In 1989, the manic-depression revived, and Rozene demanded that Pride be excused from a charity golf tournament in Albuquerque. She took him home to Dallas, where his ranting and incessant babbling resurfaced. In the middle of the night, when Rozene was unaware, he called a man from whom he often leased airplanes. The man said his staff would prepare a plane for Pride immediately. That wouldn't do. Pride wanted *Air Force One*.

Rozene had just about had it. She was unhappy with Pride's doctor, who she thought capitulated to him too often, didn't give him the proper medicine, and didn't insist that he take what he was given. She broke into tears and demanded that the doctor give her the name of the best psychiatrist in Dallas.

The doctor didn't prescribe a psychiatrist, but he did demand that Pride renew his lithium prescription. Pride resisted and told the doctor he didn't want to, that the doctor shouldn't make him.

"You're my friend," he argued to the doctor.

The doctor looked from Pride to Rozene.

"I'm not your friend," he said. "I'm your doctor."

This statement was a major victory for Rozene. Pride has been taking lithium, and has been free of depression, ever since.

"It got to where," Rozene said, "he thought the people on the television were coming after him and stuff like that. If I were going to have a mental illness, you know you can't choose your illness, but if I could and I had to have a mental illness, I'd choose manic-depression because it's so easy to control."

"With drugs?" Tom asked.

"Lithium," she said. "There's the chemical imbalance in the brain, and nobody would know to look at Pride, nobody. He didn't even want to reveal it in his book, and we [Henderson and Rozene] said, 'This is something that you really should talk about.'"

As a result of Rozene's persistence, Pride talked

about his affliction, and, said Rozene, hundreds of people have written to thank him, many of whom have returned to their medication.

Rozene Pride, to my way of thinking, saved Pride's career and his life. She had no idea that life with Pride would be laced with celebrity and melodrama when they met in a Memphis nightclub.

"Hey, I like your hair," were the first words he ever spoke to her.

Pride was living in Memphis to play minor league baseball. He spotted Rozene, handed her his telephone number, and asked her to call the next day.

She didn't. Her girlfriend did.

She asked Pride if he remembered the girl he had met last night at the Gay Hawk.

"Yes," he said.

"You said you were going to take her to the movies," the woman chided.

"Yes," Pride said. "What time do you want me to pick you up?"

"I'm not the girl."

Pride was expecting the caller to be Rozene, who had thought his approach was improper, and would never have called him. So he finally called Rozene and talked her into a first date. After all of that, he overslept and missed it.

With Rozene, that was strike two.

Rozene did not like athletes or entertainers anyhow. She thought they were stuck on themselves. She said she'd never marry anyone in either field. In Pride, she eventually got both.

"Never say never," she laughed, in her Dallas office in 1997.

On their first date, Rozene and Pride went to a movie whose title escapes her. The first thing he ever gave her was a record, "It Only Hurts for a Little While."

Shortly afterward, Pride gave Rozene's telephone number to Charley Jennings, his friend. Pride was absolutely sure that Rozene wouldn't go out with Jennings. Rozene resented Pride's inflated self-confidence and was annoyed that he passed out her number. She accepted a date with Jennings. That upset Pride, who spent the entire evening following an unsuspecting Rozene.

"Nobody owned me," said Rozene. "I was gonna show that to Pride."

The courtship had begun in July 1957. Pride, then a soldier at Ft. Chaffee, Arkansas, eventually popped the question over the long-distance wire. After a romantic summer, they were married in December. They celebrated their fortieth anniversary in 1997.

"Are you going to have a big fiftieth party?" I asked.

"Well, you know I do things differently," she said. "All of a sudden at thirty-two [years of marriage], I decided to have a big party. People said, Why didn't you have the big party on your twenty-fifth? I said, Because I didn't want to."

Rozene has always had her own life and ways. That began years earlier in her native Mississippi.

• • •

"My family had always owned their own land, but we were farmers," she recalled. "My father was a farmer but he'd also learned a trade: He was a carpenter and a painter. So my father was a very smart man, a very smart man."

"Did his children help him in his business in any way?" she was asked.

"We helped him on the farm, yeah," she remembered. "And I wanted to paint. I loved my dad when I was growing up and I thought I could paint. I wanted to paint like my dad.

"He used to build and repair houses," she continued. "And he always had the best tools that you could buy. So he had these heavy paintbrushes, the really heavy ones, and I used to bug him all the time to let me paint. So one time he gave me a heavy brush, and he said, 'Now, you've got to break [bend] your wrist, you've got to keep your arm still and break your wrist.' In just a few strokes I was cured of wanting to paint."

Rozene's actual name is Ebbie Rozene Pride. She was named after her father.

Rozene was one of four girls. Her father used psychology rather than force to discipline them. He could simply tell any of the girls he was disappointed in them, and that was ample punishment and motivation.

Jim Henderson said Rozene is the most avid female sports fan he's ever met, and the only woman he knows who can explain the infield fly rule. Rozene concedes her sports obsession and says it began on her dad's Mississippi farm.

"I'll tell you what avid fans we were," she said. "We used to run home from school, get the sports page, and read it so that when he came home and would ask us questions, we'd know the answers. As a kid, I knew every player on every major league team. There wasn't as many teams as there are now, you know? We even knew the utility players."

Rozene, to this day, regularly attends Texas Rangers baseball games and Dallas Cowboys football games. She doesn't sit in a box seat but down near the field, to be near the action. And she doesn't like to attend games with most women, as most women don't know their sports, she said.

"I don't go to the games to party," she said. "I go to watch the games."

Rozene is refreshingly honest, and that means occasionally outspoken.

Tom Carter prepared for a conversation with her by reading all he could about her. He thought she'd be pleased that he had done his homework.

With the innocent candor of a child she asked, "You know all about me, why do you have to interview me?"

He replied that he suspected she grew weary of interviewers who knew nothing about her, or about Pride, except that he was the first black to attain major success as a country singer. "I thought you'd be tired of the question about what it's like to be black and be in country music," he said.

"I hate dumb questions," she said. "Like I said to Pride, 'If one more person asks you or me how it feels to be black and in country music . . . Every reporter in England, Australia, everywhere we go, Canada, the United States—why do they continually ask that question?"

The question was current in December 1966, when Pride released his first record on RCA, "Just Between You and Me."

"I don't always answer it anymore," she said, "but Pride will, depending on his mood. He's awfully good with the press."

Rozene seems to have always done things her own way, from childhood through today. She finished high school and enrolled in a small college. "And then I looked at my situation," she said. "My father would have had three girls in college at the same time. He would have tried to struggle and do it, but I thought that was too much for my father. I need to do a trade, I decided, and then go back to school. So I dropped out of college and went to cosmetology school in Memphis."

Later, she trained as a medical technician. Still later, she and Pride moved to Montana so he could renew his minor league baseball career. There were soon two children, and Rozene simply could not find the time to return to school.

After Pride landed his RCA recording contract, everyone expected Rozene to move her family to Nashville. But she and Pride wanted to be in a city with major league sports, which Nashville did not have back then.

"We moved to Dallas and didn't know anybody," she said. "Pride had met an attorney on a plane, but we figured that if we had to leave Montana we would move to a city that, besides the sports, was centrally located. I had gone to Nashville enough at that time. There was nothing in Nashville but the music business, and when Pride was off we felt we wanted him to be off, not people calling him about songs or, you know, doing something. People that we hang out with daily in Dallas are ordinary people."

Pride's early career was managed by a man with whom Pride eventually had disagreements. Pride hates change, Rozene said, and didn't want to sever the relationship. Rozene was a part of Pride's decision making, and the manager apparently resented it.

He would give Pride contracts to sign while touring. Pride would often say he would take the documents home to Rozene for her consideration.

"'I don't manage Rozene,'" Rozene said the manager objected. "'I manage you.'"

Rozene didn't compromise, she simply stood back from a touchy situation, letting Pride know she'd be there, but only if he needed and wanted her. He did, and the manager was eventually let go during the explosive early days of Pride's career.

"The wife of an entertainer goes through a lot more than many other wives," I empathized. "Do you think it's harder to be the wife of an entertainer than, say, the wife of an accountant?"

"I don't know," was all she said, and then related the following anecdote.

Rozene and another entertainer's wife were dining at a formal affair. Another woman overheard their conversation and said, "How do you ladies make it with your husbands gone all of the time?"

Rozene didn't appreciate the question, especially after the woman repeated it twice. Then the woman said she didn't know what she would do if her husband did not come home at five every day.

Rozene knew what *she* would do.

"If I had a nine-to-five husband, I'd divorce him because I couldn't stand him around so much," Rozene told the woman, taking her by surprise.

"And then she shut up," Rozene said. "My thing was if I had a nine-to-five husband I would adjust to it, but whatever your husband does you have to adjust to it. I think that's where a lot of marriages go wrong, you have to adjust to what the situation is. Pride has made a good living for us."

"Have you ever felt like a single parent because you raised two boys and a girl when Pride was touring a lot?"

"There were days when all three of my kids were in activities in three different schools," she said. "I went to three schools for three activities. Hard, but I did it."

"Was there ever a crisis involving a child that you had to handle yourself?"

"Yeah," she said, "lots of them. At one point, both of my boys were on crutches at the same time. No matter what happened to the children, Pride would always say to me, 'What did you do to them?'"

"Did that question make you angry?"

"No," she said, "it was kinda funny because his babies couldn't get hurt by themselves, you know?"

She laughed, and went on about the time her two sons were on crutches.

"I went to pick up Pride at the airport," she said. "I took my daughter with me. She was younger. She said to her dad when he got in the car, 'Dad, Deon and Craig both are on crutches.'

"And Pride said to me, 'What did Angie just say?'

"I said, 'Nothing.' I thought, I don't want to hear this until I get home. So then when we got home and he got out of the car and he saw the boys and his first question to me was, 'What did you do to my kids?'— well, I just started laughing.

"He said, 'Angie was telling the truth,'" she went on.

"'Yes,' I said, 'but I didn't want to hear it all the way home.'"

Rozene said that when she once took two of her children to the emergency room in the same week, a nurse joked that the hospital didn't give family rates. One child had a hairline fracture, and the other had a concussion. Rozene handled both just fine.

Another time, one of the boys taunted the other to throw a baseball faster. The result: The receiving boy caught the ball in the mouth.

Pride, Rozene said, went to pieces.

"We were all getting ready to go down to one of those arenas because there was a heavyweight fight," she remembered. "We were going to see it on the big screen. Well, Pride was just all over Craig [the son who threw the ball]. Well, Craig felt so bad anyhow. So finally I said to Pride, 'You, everybody, just get out of here and go to the fight and I'll handle this myself.'"

Her youngest son was bleeding profusely. She wrapped a towel around his head, fastened him in his seat belt, and sped to the hospital. She had saved the situation—again.

The pressures of motherhood began for Rozene in 1958 when her first child was one year old. She, Pride, and their baby were involved in an automobile accident in a southern state. Authorities advised that they take their car to a gasoline station owned by a white man. They left it for repair. When they returned, the car had been stripped of many of its accessories and parts.

The newlyweds were devastated. They were poor, and that old car was their most valuable possession. Now it was gone.

Their baby, still in diapers, began to cry because of hunger. Pride walked to a whites-only restaurant and instinctively went to the back door. It didn't matter. The proprietor would not give milk to the father of a black baby.

Tom asked Rozene about her married life as a de facto single woman.

"What about when you were newlyweds and Pride was gone a lot? Did you ever worry about the temptations that might be afforded him by other women?"

"Yeah," she said simply, "but what could I do about it?"

"So is that something you just accept?"

"Yeah," she said, "or either trust him, you know?"

"Do you think he's always been trustworthy?"

"I don't think that's a fair question," she said, "because only he could answer that."

"It's not something you have discussed?"

"I'm sure every marriage discusses it," she said. "But I mean, the UPS deliveryman could do the same thing."

"What would you describe as the favorite recollection of your marriage?"

"Oh, there's been a lot of good ones," she said, "like the birth of our children, seeing when they do something wonderful, but between Pride and me, I think there was a trip we took to Hawaii one time, the first time we went together and left the children. I thought that was wonderful."

"Do you have any reservations about your children entering the entertainment industry, or do you wish they'd do something more stable?"

"It doesn't matter to me what they do," she said. "I just want my kids to be happy."

"You seem like a wonderfully well-adjusted person. You don't seem as if you would get hysterical easily."

"I don't," she said. "Pride is probably more emotional than I am. I try to pray the Serenity prayer. I really like it. Like if I get stuck in traffic or something, there is nothing I can do about it. I have learned, I guess partly with age, that the things you can't do nothing about you've got to accept."

Mrs. Charley Pride is on the board of directors of one of the top five minority-owned banks in the United States. She and Pride once owned majority stock in the bank. She said she learned a lot about finance, and it improved her ability to handle the family money, which she has done for years.

She's constantly trying to explain her financial decisions to Pride, but he's not overly interested in hearing about it. He trusts her implicitly.

Now that they had sold their share of the bank, she said, "What I want to do is simplify my life. I'm at the stage now where I want to pick up and go when I get ready. If I want to stay in bed and watch tennis, I want to do it. I'm tired of the decision making. I want to stop."

In the summer of 1997, Charley Pride was given the Pioneer Award by The Nashville Network and *Music City News* magazine. It is the network's and the magazine's most prestigious award, presented each year during Fan Fair, the weeklong gala in Nashville where country fans are allowed to mix socially with the stars.

Pride had no idea he was going to receive it, as no nominees are announced. Officials with the awards show called Rozene and asked if she could trick Pride into coming to Nashville to be surprised on network television.

She told Pride he needed to go to Nashville to

mingle more than he customarily does with people in the music business, and to honor Neal McCoy, who was nominated for another award. McCoy is a young singer who is close to the Pride family.

Pride reluctantly complied. When his name was announced, he was visibly astonished. He was deeply touched.

Grand Ole Opry star Johnny Russell, after the awards show, was listening to Rozene tell how she had kept Pride totally in the dark about going to Nashville to receive the award.

"Well, Charley," Russell said, "you know if Rozene kept that secret from you that long, you'd better find out what else she's keeping from you."

The three laughed a lot.

14

I don't know Mrs. Kenny (Wanda) Rogers. I read about her courtship with Kenny and about her wedding performed inside a barn on Kenny's five-hundred-acre estate. Tom Carter drove three hundred miles to interview her on my behalf. I didn't go because George doesn't like it when I'm away overnight.

Wanda and I have many mutual friends who speak highly of her. Tom returned with a story that I think is unusual. So he and I wrote it.

A marriage till death do us part wouldn't have gotten beyond the first date if Kenny Rogers hadn't carried personal identification. He makes a case for the charge card company that always urges people to never leave home without it.

It seems Kenny entered an Atlanta restaurant with a date in 1993 where Wanda was a hostess. The next day he called the restaurant, gave his telephone number to an employee, and asked that he relay it to Wanda. The employee complied, and Wanda immediately threw the number in the trash.

"I thought it was a practical joke," she said on the one-month anniversary of their marriage. "They were always playing jokes on me at that restaurant, like telling me to take a drink to a handsome man who hadn't even ordered one. So when they told me Kenny Rogers wanted me to call, I didn't take them seriously."

Employees retrieved the number and insisted they were sincere. Kenny Rogers, they claimed, wanted to talk to the attractive brunette who had attended him the previous night.

Frustrated and apprehensive, Wanda called the number, which was answered by an electronic voice. Convinced she'd been duped, she nonetheless left her number.

Then her phone rang. The caller said he was Kenny Rogers. Wanda said the distinctiveness of his speaking voice convinced her it was him.

He asked her to dinner, then he asked her to come to his hotel room. She had repeatedly vowed to herself that if asked, she wouldn't go. Not under any circumstances.

Once they were inside the room, Kenny gave her a compact disc and a book of his photographs. They sat in a semi-darkened suite overlooking Lenox Square, arguably the swankiest shopping mall in Atlanta. All was going fine.

Then Wanda decided to bolt. Something about the way light leaked onto his face told her the man beside her was an imposter, a Kenny Rogers look-alike.

"But I gave you these gifts," Kenny argued.

"Oh yeah, anybody could have bought these anywhere. They don't prove you're really Kenny Rogers."

Silence.

"Show me some identification!"

More silence. Kenny Rogers, one of the world's most recognizable men, realized the woman he'd wined, dined, and showered with gifts was serious—and scared. She didn't know who she was with or what he might attempt. She was only certain that she was several feet away from a solid wooden door with three locks she had turned. There was no way to flee.

"I want to see some identification," she repeated.

Kenny produced a driver's license with his name and photograph. Wanda was satisfied, and started to breathe a sigh of relief.

"Now *I* want to see *your* identification," Kenny said. "How do I know you're as old as you say?"

She had told him that she was twenty-six.

So she presented proof of her age. He decided she was old enough for a then fifty-six-year-old man, and let her stay.

She eventually toured with him. Four years and a million miles later, she became his sixth wife.

She arose on June 1, 1997, the date of their wedding, and faced a cloudless sky radiant with sunshine. There was no reason to think it might rain, but Wanda had a gut feeling.

She told Kenny she was overhauling the wedding plans. She wanted to tear down the outdoor decorations and move the wedding inside the barn.

He resisted, thinking her notions were wacky, but offered to compromise by having half of the ceremony outside and half inside.

She wouldn't budge. The discussion became an argument, just twelve hours before their first night as man and wife.

Kenny relented.

She called for members of Kenny's road and domestic crew to move indoors a gazebo, carpet, tables, approximately two hundred chairs, and more.

The workmen began at 8:00 A.M. and finished at 5:30 P.M., one hour before guests arrived for a prewedding reception.

"Men don't mind being wet, but women hate it," she said. "I didn't care how it looked outside—something told me it would be raining by the time of our evening wedding. I *knew* it would rain."

It did. In bucketfuls. Wanda's intuition saved the ceremony.

Like many Nashville wives (Kenny records and has business operations in Nashville), she travels with Kenny almost everywhere. She said he thinks he's lost without her, and she's positive she's lost without him. He is both of their lives.

"Is there any part of your life that does not involve Kenny Rogers?" Tom asked.

"No," she said, "there's not. There really isn't."

Wanda believes in her man throughout—in both behavior and words. She personifies the stand-by-your-man mentality.

Kenny is now sixty-one, Wanda thirty-one.

"I honestly never think about the age difference," she said.

Neither does she think about the version of any story that isn't his.

"I believe him," she said.

Her remark was in reference to a sex scandal that rocked Kenny's career in 1992, less than a year before their first date.

Back in 1985, Kenny had been voted top male musical performer three times in the People's Choice Awards, a public popularity poll. As one of eight children, he grew up in a thirty-five-dollar-a-month federal housing complex. He eventually formed the group Kenny Rogers and the First Edition and earned $125,000 a year, but he was left $65,000 in debt when the band broke up.

A champion of tenacity, he came back in a way so dramatic that it is virtually unprecedented in the annals of show business. In 1977, he recorded "Lucille," and the resulting hurricane of popularity was out of this world. Kenny was along for the whirl. He sold $250 million worth of records in five years. The first of his four *Gambler* movies was the highest rated TV movie of the 1979–1980 season. Besides his Georgia estate, he owned a home in Malibu and another in Beverly Hills. There were real estate holdings, including property in pricey Los Angeles. He flew from show to show in his private aircraft.

In the 1990s he built a seventeen-room home in

the side of a mountain in Branson, Missouri, along with a namesake theater.

His multimillion-dollar empire was felled by a twenty-dollar telephone call.

Kenny had an 800 number of which his fourth wife—of fifteen years—Marianne, was unaware. Women from around the nation were given the number. Kenny reportedly invited women to call the 800 number to hear explicit conversation.

Two women recorded Kenny's telephone voice and made it public. In 1992 the tapes were aired in part on a nationally televised show. Kenny appeared the next night on *Larry King Live* to explain himself and to ask the people of Branson and the nation not to hold his behavior against him.

But they did.

Attendance fell off at his Branson theater. Patronage at his Kenny Rogers Roasters chain of chicken restaurants diminished. The Nashville restaurant, near the tourist-laden Music Row, closed in 1997. Kenny's Georgia mansion, complete with an eighteen-hole golf course, was put up for sale in 1996. By 1997, the asking price reportedly had been lowered twice. And there were no takers as of this writing.

People close to Kenny confided that he was in dire financial straits.

Kenny was sued by three Texas women who alleged he had coaxed them into having telephone sex, according to an article in the February 8, 1993, issue of *People* magazine.

One woman, an actress, contended that Kenny lured her to a hotel room with the promise of an audition, then made sexual advances. She said he was nothing like the public perceived him, and called him sick.

Wanda doesn't believe any of it. Kenny has told her it was untrue.

She was asked how many girls had taken action against Kenny.

"There were two," she said. "One backed out, though, right, and this got—hurt the other girl. Her attorney came forward and said, 'Oh, this was a complete extortion case because she had told me she was going to do this.' I just believed [Kenny]. When you get to know Kenny, you—I just didn't think he had a hidden agenda at all, and none of that [scandal] bothered me."

Wanda, in a nutshell, is young, beautiful, and believing. She was born in Valdosta, Georgia, near the Georgia/Florida line. She has a twin sister, Tonia, who is her only sibling. They're almost physically identical in every way, and Kenny had to learn to tell them apart. The lesson took three days.

"We grew up playing softball, basketball. My dad tried to make us into boys. We were tomboys, and we grew up riding motorcycles, and we did tap dance, ballet, piano lessons for eight years. We had to do it as a pair. We went off to college as a pair, we had our first job at Kentucky Fried Chicken together. I mean, we did everything, college, everything we did together, which was great because she's a built-in best friend." She is co-dependent with Tonia. Kenny says they have a rubber-band relationship. If they don't see each other regularly, they snap into each other's presence as if rapidly drawn by elastic.

"Is she married?" Wanda was asked.

"No."

"What if Kenny had met her first?"

"I don't want to think about that," Wanda replied.

"Is your sister working?"

"She's a dental hygienist in Atlanta," Wanda said. "That's one of the things I went to school for. I started out in nursing, then I decided I wanted to be a schoolteacher, and then I went to dental hygiene school with Tonia and I only lacked one quarter finishing that and we had clinic in school and I would just cry and pray, 'Oh, I hope my patient doesn't show up.' So I kinda knew I was in the wrong profession, so I didn't finish it because I knew I'd be stuck doing that, and then I started public relations."

Then she married a commercial gambler, dropped out of college, and moved to England.

"I was probably twenty-four when I moved to England, and I got married to a British guy—a very, very nice guy. He was a bookmaker, a professional gambler, and it was a fun lifestyle. He was a bookie at the dog tracks. It was really fun."

Gambling is legal in England. Homesickness is legal everywhere. Wanda was homesick for America, her sister, and friends, but her husband could not legally practice his craft back in America. So Wanda left him and returned to the States.

Her parents were chagrined about the divorce, but then they'd been unhappy about the marriage, too. They belong to the conservative Pentecostal church. Wanda's first husband, in their minds, practiced sin for a living.

So after divorcing a literal gambler, she wound up marrying a figurative one. Kenny's stage nickname is "The Gambler."

She said her parents initially disapproved of Kenny.

"They disapproved, because of the age difference mainly, and because of Kenny being a celebrity," she explained. "But when they met him and they were around him—he's so down-to-earth, and you just feel different about him. . . ."

"Was there *ever* a time when the age difference was a consideration to you?" Tom asked.

"This probably sounds strange but I *never* feel the age difference," Wanda affirmed. "I mean, because I feel we're very—so compatible."

She and Kenny have discussed having children but he doesn't want them at his age. She doesn't want to surrender her independence to the responsibility of motherhood.

"I know that sounds selfish, but it [having a child] would change my lifestyle so much, and I enjoy the traveling and the freedom."

Wanda's day begins around 7:30 A.M., as does Kenny's. She said she feels fortunate that both are early risers.

Her first order of business is usually a tennis lesson.

"And when Kenny gets up he usually mows fairways," she said, without being asked. If she mentions what she does, she automatically seems to make an analogy to Kenny.

He rides a tractor, she said, to mow the fairways on their private golf course, "and he'll use the other lawnmower to cut the regular grass."

Later, it's in-home physical fitness class for Wanda, unofficially taught by a friend who teaches makeup application and step classes. Kenny doesn't participate, but others on his staff do. There appears to be team spirit on the sprawling farm.

The routine is enacted about five days a week, as Kenny performs concerts on weekends, and Wanda, of course, attends. On the road, the two relax with tennis. They take a tennis professional on the trips, Wanda said.

Back at home, Wanda often spends afternoons shopping in Atlanta, perhaps forty-five minutes away.

"I lived in Atlanta for seven years," she said, "so all of my friends are there."

"What has been your most romantic moment with Kenny Rogers?"

"I guess it is one moment when we were living in Las Vegas," she recalled. "I'd go visit him in Las

Vegas, and each time I'd leave some clothes, and say, 'I'll leave this because I'll wear it the next time I come back.' Gradually his closet was full. Anyway, I was real skeptical about moving in. I don't know if you know Lake Powell, but it's at the northern tip of the Grand Canyon. Well, we'd just cooked our dinner on the houseboat and we were lying under the stars. It was like a sky full of—like a starburst. We'd finally gotten to where, I mean, I was living with him. We had a monogamous relationship and I guess I felt, while lying under those stars, that nothing else mattered."

"When you were young, if you were like most young girls, you probably had a fantasy man. Is Kenny like that fantasy?"

"Yeah," she answered quickly. "He's exactly what I would have wanted. He's very, very compassionate, very witty, and most of all he has this respect level for other people that is so extreme. I've never been around another person in my life who has so much respect for other people. That's very important."

When asked to recall any quarrels that she and Kenny have had, Wanda mentioned nothing specific. She simply assumed the blame.

"I think sometimes I can be a spoiled brat," she said. "I can pout and throw a temper tantrum and it does not work."

She attributed that to immaturity and cited the age difference as the cause, despite her earlier contention that age has never made a difference. She doesn't think they have problems because Kenny is older, but because she's younger.

"What bugs me most about it is what the tabloids say and the big deal everyone else makes about it because they almost make it seem really bad, but the truth is Kenny was married to Marianne for fifteen years, twelve to fifteen years. I think he had a really long-term relationship there. His first wife was when he was nineteen and it was real short-lived, and his second wife he was married to for like eight or nine years, and then the third wife was very short—like a year or two. So two of those marriages were such a flash in the pan that, you know—everybody makes mistakes—but it goes on record."

"Marianne lived here," Tom noted. "Did you change the house?"

Wanda said that Kenny loves to decorate and changed the home's entire interior for his newest bride.

"It felt strange at first, you know, with their [Kenny and Marianne's] staff that they'd had for years. That felt kind of strange."

"So you were the newcomer among people who had worked for his last wife?"

"Right, right. But I tell you, everyone has made me feel so comfortable. I'm really close to everyone now. At first it was a little strange. Whenever we saw our therapist, this is so funny, the one thing I hadn't thought about was coming here and I saw him before we came here and he said, 'Moving into this house—Wanda, I don't think you have thought about it. That staff has been with Kenny and Marianne for twelve years. You're going to be moving your stuff into her closet.' He's the one that brought all of this stuff to my mind, and I left there scared to death. I'm kind of happy-go-lucky until something hits me in the face. I left there scared, and Kenny said, 'Oh no, we're not ever going back to him.' "

But they did.

Wanda lived with Kenny in Kenny and Marianne's house for about eighteen months before marriage made her the first lady of the manor. She stopped short of saying whether she slept where Marianne had slept.

"You mentioned monogamy. Is that important to you?"

"Yes, yes," she said. "It's very important. When I was just starting to date him, that wasn't very important. I'd gotten back in college, I was working, and I was really just having fun with my friends. But as we started seeing each other—about eight months into it—we really started getting monogamous. It really felt nice, it did, starting to tie the knot."

As of this writing, Kenny was rehearsing a Christmas show. He planned to take it on a tour to end on Broadway at Christmas in 1999, Wanda said. The script calls for part of the cast to wear animal costumes.

"I may be a teddy bear," Wanda said. "This is a

toy story, and it's life-size toys that come to life so I'm probably just going to stand because I don't really sing. But I don't want to wear a hood. I think it will be hot and miserable. But I've got to decide if I want to do that because I don't want to be the spoiled brat on the set."

"Did you ever graduate from college?" she was asked.

"I did not, and that's one thing that bugs me too," she said. Kenny asked her why she needs a degree, and she said it would just make her "feel good."

She was asked if she'd return to her public relations curriculum. She won't, because she has changed her major field of study for the fourth time—to psychology.

"We have a therapist in Atlanta," she said. "And he's a psychologist and he has two students that are getting their—what do you call it? They've graduated and now they're doing their residency under him. And so he said, 'When you get this degree, I'll set you up in a little office right here and you could just play around with a few patients.' A lightbulb went off. I thought that might be interesting."

"Do you take this marriage one day at a time?"

She said she did, and intended to do so forever.

She was asked how she intended to make a marriage permanent with a man who'd walked down the matrimonial aisle five times previously.

"We have a thing that we do and we've done

since I can remember," she said. "And this is maybe kind of silly but it's big to us—to start every day with a big hug before you get up. That's our big thing. Even if you have to go to the restroom or something, you come back, and you hug."

15

The late Hank Williams had two wives. Audrey is dead and a lot of people wrongly assume the other, Billy Jean, is too. She has divorced two husbands and buried two others, along with other immediate family members. In 1980, after her father's passing, she sort of eased into obscurity in the public's mind. I think a lot of people assumed Billy Jean died a quiet death.

She is very much alive, and anything but quiet.

She lives in Louisiana and probably prefers that I not mention the town. Her niece said Billy Jean sleeps until 5:00 P.M. daily and doesn't like to deal with day people.

George Jones still calls Hank Williams the greatest country singer-songwriter who ever lived, almost a half century after Hank's death. The former Miss Billy Jean Jones was married to Hank for two months and thirteen days. The day of Hank's funeral, she was asked for a date by the late Johnny Horton. She said she waited about a month before accepting, then was married to Horton for seven years.

Williams died from drug-induced heart failure at age twenty-nine in 1953. Horton perished in a car wreck in 1960.

I didn't talk to Billy Jean and Tom Carter didn't talk much. She did most of the talking. I was astonished at what she had to say, and I'm not astonished easily.

Following are highlights from the one woman to marry two of the biggest country stars of the 1950s or, for that matter, of all time. Given her spunk, I'm not sure too many eligible male country stars of the 1990s are safe.

The former Mrs. Hank Williams, Sr. suspects Hank may have been killed by his own mother. That bombshell has never been previously published in the forty-five years since Hank's death. The widow never got even, but she got a taste of revenge. She physically beat up Hank's mother during a wake while Hank lay in state a few feet away.

"I think she would have rather seen him dead than married to me," said Mrs. Billy Jean Horton, Hank's wife at the time of his death.

"Do you really think Hank was killed by his own mother?" Tom asked.

"Hank's mother gave him shots the whole time during Christmas [he died on New Year's Day, 1953]," she said. "I never did trust those things [shots].

"I told her at the time, I said, 'I don't know what the hell you're giving him but it makes him goofy,' and I didn't know, but I know Hank—when she popped him with those shots, he didn't like it, but there was nothing you could say to her.

"I know she gave him shots and also she paid for the prescription," she went on. "She called Toby Marshall, who was not a doctor."

Billy Jean said she told Marshall he was a fraud.

"I says, 'If you are a damn doctor, I'm a Negro aviator.' I said, 'You are not a doctor.'

"Hank would fall out and he'd foam, bright foam would come out of his mouth, and I'd have to sit up and keep that foam from choking him. It would knock him out okay but as I learned on down the line at that guy's [Marshall's] trial that truly he was a, you know, ex-con that went back to learn how to write those prescriptions and was doing so on a stolen pad for chloral hydrate, which is the old Mickey Finn."

After Hank's death, Billy Jean received a bill for $736.39 from "Dr. Toby Marshall," who had, in fact, prescribed sedatives for Hank. In the end, of course, Marshall turned out to be a paroled forger rather than a doctor, and admitted under oath that he had violated federal narcotics laws by giving Hank twenty-four grains of chloral hydrate, a sedative for alcoholics that is also a heart depressant.

Hank's funeral was attended by more than 25,000 people, according to the newspaper in Montgomery, Alabama, his birthplace. Ernest Tubb, Red Foley, and Roy Acuff, three of the day's biggest country stars, sang.

"It was a fiasco," said Billy Jean. "I said the sons of bitches didn't even like him, they wouldn't even talk to him when he was alive. They turned out because they knew it would probably be the biggest gig they ever played, and it was."

She said that in a newspaper article, and signed her name. Lawyers for the publication feared a libel suit.

Billy Jean feared nothing.

"I said, 'I welcome all comers,'" she said. "'You all come and hop on this bird because I'll fight you quick.' All I did was tell the truth, and I really meant it. I said I'll live long enough to be big enough to ignore every one of the sons of bitches that wouldn't help Hank when he was alive. I'll live to tell every one of them to kiss my ass. Because I went on to marry another guy. And he was big into stardom. And when he got killed, I just went on."

The former Billy Jean Jones's matrimonial ties to the luminaries were indirectly initiated the night she visited the Grand Ole Opry in Nashville in 1952 with aspiring country singer Faron Young. Faron, like Billy Jean, was from Louisiana. Both were singers, and Faron seriously pursued a career. He had aspirations to become a member of the Opry.

A country singer who was granted membership into the Opry in the 1950s was like a stand-up comedian landing a job as host of *The Tonight Show* today. Both slots are certifications of having indisputably made it.

Billy Jean, then eighteen, left her infant daughter in the temporary care of her mother in Bossier City while visiting Nashville with Faron. Going to the

Opry with Faron might mean a ticket out of her impoverished plight into the bright lights of country music's Tin Pan Alley, Nashville, Tennessee. She isn't sure she was ready to get out of Louisiana, but she was ready to get a leg up on life.

She lived with her mother until age sixteen and, she said, she continued to sass and be difficult. Although she was not pregnant, her mother made her get married, she said.

"I lipped off at my mother when I was sixteen," Billy Jean recalled, from her Louisiana home. "I smarted off one time too many, and she made me get married. She said, 'You pick one of those guys you been dating 'cause you're fixing to get married and get out of my face.' I didn't want to do that 'cause I thought I was a big shot. So she said, 'I'm going to show you what a big shot ain't.'"

Billy Jean's mother, a barroom bouncer, was tough. Billy said her mom once knocked out the mayor of Bossier City. Billy Jean was out of the house and married within three days after her mother ordered her departure.

"I got married and I didn't have a clue what made you pregnant," she continued. "I didn't even know what the guy [her husband] was doing when he was up there [having intercourse]. I says, 'You know that half a bologna sandwich that's in the icebox? Let's go get it, want to?' Well, you know what that will do to a hard? But he must have come back. 'Cause I got pregnant in the first week and I didn't know how in the hell I'd got there."

Divorce followed, although Billy Jean is ambiguous about whether it preceded her dating of Hank Williams.

On her first visit to Nashville with Faron, Billy Jean sat in a section reserved for entertainers' guests. While awaiting Faron's Opry appearance, she was enthralled by the most magnetic country singer of the day—Hank Williams.

She said Hank looked up at her as he was taking bows and making his way off the stage. She had read about his turbulent marriage to Audrey Williams.

Hank soon found his way to a seat beside Billy Jean.

She said Hank asked her if she were married and that she said no.

" 'Well, ole Hank's going to marry you,' " she quoted Hank as saying.

Billy Jean said Hank told his friend, the late Minnie Pearl, to go get that kid from Louisiana (Faron).

" 'Faron,' " she said Hank asked, " 'are you going to marry this girl?' " Faron said he was not, and Hank affirmed that *he* was.

Billy Jean and Hank Williams, minus spouses, had their first date that night.

She said she was worried about Faron, since she had been taught always to depart an event with the man with whom she had arrived. But Hank told Faron, she said, to take his date, and he would take Faron's.

So the men switched women. Faron drove

Hank's original date beside him in the front seat, while Hank rode in the back with Billy Jean.

Why did Faron consent to the swap?

"Because Faron knew that if he wanted to get on the Opry full-time all Hank had to say was you don't get on the Opry," Billy Jean said. "Faron was a kid, and he didn't back-talk Hank. We thought Hank was the old guy and he was nine years older than us."

Hank and Billy Jean sat in the car while Faron and Hank's original date went into a nightclub. At this time Billy Jean was living in Shreveport, Louisiana, and so, coincidentally, was Hank. She said she told Hank that night that she frequently saw him drive past her modest house. She said she recalls to this day how sad he looked each time he passed.

"I told him I used to see him ride by my house every day and he had those pretty brown eyes and the way he glared, it just made you feel sorry for him," she said. "He just had that haunted look.

"I'd tell my mama—you know girls, they've got big dreams—and I said, 'Mama, one of these days I'm going to marry that man.' Yeah. That big ole white cowboy hat. I said, 'I'm going to marry that man.'"

Hank paid ninety dollars for legal fees to garner Billy Jean's divorce, and a small fortune in assets for his divorce from Audrey.

He was fired from the Grand Ole Opry in September 1952, due to missed appearances and misbehavior that was drug- and alcohol-induced. Buddy Killen, a bass player for Hank, talked in his 1993 autobiography, *By the Seat of My Pants,* about seeing Hank inject drugs into his veins.

A month after his Opry dismissal, Hank married Billy Jean on the stage of the New Orleans Auditorium as part of a show.

"That was kind of like a fairy tale that you'd see in the movies," she said. "We married secretly out in the woods the night before in Minden, Louisiana—thirty miles out of town."

Hank was afraid that Audrey would come to New Orleans and make a scene to attract press that would spoil his marriage to Billy Jean, Billy Jean explained. At the suggestion of a friend, Hank and Billy Jean decided the New Orleans ceremony would be only a formality.

After the marriage in the woods, Hank and Billy Jean started to town in her brother's car. They ran out of gasoline.

"So Hank got out there, and the first car that came by he flags him down, him with his rhinestone suit and big old cowboy hat," Billy Jean said. "The car stops and Hank is so grateful that he invites the guy to spend the night with us."

"On your wedding night?"

"That's the way Hank was," she said. "Hank didn't think about things like that, nor really did I. Whatever he wanted to do, you know, and my mind didn't run on sex, that didn't cross my mind."

So Hank, Billy Jean, and the good Samaritan—just the three of them—spent the wedding night at Hank's apartment in Bossier City. "Hank was grateful and it didn't make me any difference. Hell, you know, whatever he wanted to do was all right with me."

"Where did you eventually live?" she was asked.

"We had a house that we rented in Bossier City for one hundred dollars a month," she said. "But we lived wherever Hank wanted to at the time. You never knew where home was with Hank. Hank was where he was at the time, just exactly like George Jones was. You'd hear rumors that Hank was going back to Nashville because he was contracted there, and then you'd hear rumors that said he couldn't go back to Nashville because he was contracted somewhere else. Hank didn't care about no damn contract. Hank would be where he wanted to be."

"Did you eventually make some of the personal appearance shows with Hank?" she was asked.

She said she quit her job as a telephone company operator to accompany Hank to shows. She said he would not go unless she went with him. ——

Her biggest battle with Hank, as has been previously publicized, was to keep him sober. She frequently had him admitted to a hospital or sanitarium and bid him a tearful good-bye. By the time she walked to her car, he was often sitting on the hood.

She said he would remove intravenous needles intended to nourish him and simply walk out of the medical facility.

"'Ole Hank is ready to go home,' he'd tell me. 'Don't leave ole Hank in this place.'"

Hank had a reputation for destroying property,

and occasionally people, when drinking. Billy Jean was asked if she ever saw that firsthand.

"No," she insisted. "I wasn't Audrey. You didn't shoot up my house or tear up my house. You didn't hit me either. Hank knew that."

She said she had additional difficulty with people who wanted to cater to Hank Williams. She said she often checked him into hotel rooms where she was positive there was no alcohol. She said she would lock him inside the room, but that he would call the front desk and offer one hundred dollars for a quart of whiskey. She said Hank would lower a makeshift rope, perhaps woven from curtains, holding money for a bellhop waiting below. The bellhop would unfasten the cash and attach the whiskey. When Billy Jean returned to the room, she often found Hank passed out.

Once, suspecting that Hank had hidden liquor inside his room, she told him good-bye and walked out, only to re-enter quickly. Hank was on his knees, looking for something under the bed.

"'I'm only looking for my shoes,'" she quoted Hank as saying.

"Your shoes are on your feet," she said.

"Oh," he replied, and sheepishly pulled out a six-pack of beer. A six-pack would make him drunk, since he weighed so little, and was hopelessly addicted to alcohol. She said he often went days without solid food, sustained only by the vitamins and minerals within blended whiskey.

Billy Jean could teach a class on the handling of drunks. She said one never argues with a drunk when he's drunk. One instead coddles the drunk in an effort to get him to go to sleep. One only talks seriously about the alcoholism when the drunk is sober and not hungover.

I used to use the same technique with George.

A ringing telephone interrupted Billy Jean. She assumed the call was for her daughter. "I wish my daughter would not be over here," she said. "That's probably that old ugly boy looking for her and I'm fixing to take the phone off the hook so it won't ring no more. The ugliest guys turn up over here."

Billy Jean's recollections about married life with Hank Williams were drawn from only two months and thirteen days.

She remembers as much about living with his death as living with the man.

"Do you remember when you first heard the news that he was dead?" she was asked.

"Right," she said. "I answered the phone at my mother's. I was staying with them [her parents]. I was staying with them because it was into New Year's Eve and stuff. So the operator asked to talk to my dad, Lieutenant Jones [a police officer]. Hank's chauffeur was calling for my dad.

"So I says, 'Operator, this call is from West Virginia, it's probably my husband and he's probably drunk and maybe in jail and he wants to talk to me.'

"So she says, 'Well, is Lieutenant Jones there?' And she says, 'Let me talk to him.'

"So I said, 'Daddy, it's ole Hank.' I said, 'He must be in jail again, because if he'd get in jail he'd call Daddy and Daddy, being a policeman, could get him out in them days. And it got awfully quiet. And I could tell by the way Daddy was talking that it was not good. And I was sitting up in the middle of the bed by this time. And Daddy hung up and started to the bed and I can remember I started screaming.

" 'Daddy,' I speculated, 'Hank has slid off a mountain.' We'd been up in West Virginia before and I never liked going up there because of the mountains. [Hank was en route to a show through the mountains.] And Daddy started to cry, and he said, 'No, he's dead.'

"I refused to believe it," she continued. "I said, 'Give me that number. I'm going to call back,' and I called back so many times. So I called the undertaker. I knew from being around the police business that they had to do autopsies. And to do an autopsy they had to put fluid in you. I knew if they put that fluid in him, he wouldn't wake up.

"See, he had a habit," she went on. "Sometimes he'd go to sleep and I would be around and I could wake him up. So I told that undertaker, don't touch him until I get there. He's not dead, he's asleep. He does this all of the time and I can wake him up."

Billy Jean's father rented a taxi to drive her from Bossier City to Roanoke, Virginia. Hank had been on the way to Canton, Ohio, for a show on New Year's Day. His chauffeur, Charles Carr, had stopped the car because he thought Hank was sleeping unusually soundly. He had touched Hank's hand and it was lifeless.

Billy Jean, her father, and a driver trod slowly over ice-slickened roads adjacent to treacherous mountain slopes.

Hank's mother, Lillian Stone, had arrived earlier.

"The old lady had chartered a plane and beat me to the body," Billy Jean said. "She took all of his personal possessions. She took his car, and I never saw either of our cars again."

"Did she dislike you?" Billy Jean was asked.

"She didn't like me at all," she answered. "We fought all of the time because she didn't want me married to Hank. I cut her funds off. She didn't need any more funds. She had more money than anybody did."

Billy Jean stressed that Hank made a great deal of money, but squandered it.

"Hank's mother was an old bastard that died of the uglies," Billy Jean said. She said she hated Hank's late mother.

She said the mother took Hank's body to her living room in Montgomery, Alabama, Hank's hometown. Billy Jean went there without invitation.

While Hank's body lay in state, Billy Jean encountered Hank's mother in the bathroom. He had not been embalmed for forty-eight hours. People were weeping and pacing. Meanwhile, Billy Jean was pounding Hank's mother in the head inside the woman's own bathroom.

"Two doors to the bathroom and I don't guess it had no locks on them because I came in one door and she came in the other and I got up on the commode to slap her," Billy Jean said.

She said Lillian weighed about two hundred thirty pounds and was six feet, five inches tall. Lillian had run a boardinghouse and alleged bordello in Montgomery.

"My daddy heard this commotion and man, here they all come 'cause they were waiting on it," she went on. "They just knew if we met the flame would commence. I came up mean. I wouldn't pick on you but I wouldn't take nothin'. And you know, I didn't marry Hank for money."

"He didn't leave you any, did he?" she was asked.

"But he didn't know the difference," she said. "He didn't know anything about wills and crap like that. He was a boy. He was a boy that never had a childhood."

She said that she, nineteen when Hank died, was a "dumb ole country girl" who didn't know her rights. She said she would have never consented to Hank's burial in Montgomery, Alabama. She mistakenly thought that his mother had all legal rights pertaining to decisions in the wake of Hank's death.

"The old lady [Hank's mother] had money and Audrey had money," Billy Jean said. "All I could do was get my daddy to pay my way back home to Louisiana from the funeral in Montgomery on a Greyhound bus."

And that's where she stayed until she wed her next celebrity.

• • •

Billy Jean dated Johnny Horton for nine months before they were married. The marriage produced two children and a grandchild who lives with Billy Jean today. While Horton was never one of the true influentials of country music, he was far more than a mere matrimonial consolation.

Horton's "The Battle of New Orleans" was released in 1959 and held the number-one slot in *Billboard* for ten weeks, and was charted for twenty-one. "North to Alaska" was a number-one tune for five weeks, was charted for twenty-two, and was the title song from a soundtrack for a film starring John Wayne. There were several other top-ten tunes.

Life with Johnny was as different from life with Hank as a fiddle is from a steel guitar.

"It was a drastic switch," said Billy Jean. "Horton didn't drink at all. So for a while it was a relief, but then he was—after a while it got to where you were wondering which was the worst because he was overly religious. Then he went into his spiritualist kick. He and Merle Kilgore and Johnny Cash got on that damn crystal ball and, you know, that's too spooky for me."

"They would read crystal balls?"

"Oh God, they had séances, they were having séances and they really believed they could call the dead. So that was causing us a little problem. If he hadn't grown out if it, I would have left him."

She said that Horton was financially irresponsible. Billy Jean takes pride in her fiscal responsibility, even to this day, and when Horton wanted to quit show business to run a fishing camp, it was the final straw.

"He wanted to move to a fishing camp," she said. "He never liked music, never. So I says, 'Well, let me tell you something, pal. I've busted my ass and I've put every dime that I made into you and had kids and now we have a nice home and if you think that I'm going to throw this away and move to a fishing camp, you'd better get a grip.'

"If you had left it up to Horton," she said, "he would have never done anything but fish and hunt."

Her recollections of a two-month, thirteen-day marriage to Hank Williams were more plentiful than her memoirs of seven years with Horton. But, as with Hank, she remembered vividly how she heard that Horton was dead.

"My daddy told me, and again, it was in the middle of the night," she said. "I was asleep. I was expecting Johnny home at about 5:30 in the morning because we were going hunting. I didn't hunt with Johnny all of the time because if you hunt with him, prepare not to eat, don't take any coffee, and don't have to pee."

"But your daddy told you that Horton had been killed in a car accident?"

"Right," she said, redirecting her thoughts. "I was at home, naturally, with the kids. I didn't travel a lot with Johnny because I had three kids [two by Horton] and we bought a new home after Johnny hit and I really liked to stay at home. In my day, you took care of your house and your kids."

"But about Horton's death?"

"So anyway," she went on, "my daddy rang the doorbell, and it was too early to be Johnny. It was about 2:30 in the morning. It was the front door and if it had been Johnny he would have rang the back door if he had forgotten his key. So I knew something was wrong. I went to the door and through the glass I could see my daddy in his police uniform. And a minister. I opened the door and started backing up and running and screaming. I can remember my daddy caught me. My daddy held me and we cried and cried and the louder we cried the louder the preacher prayed."

"Do you remember the funeral?"

"Oh Christ, everybody from the governor on was there," she said. "My house was filled up by the night when it came over the news that he was dead and I couldn't have gotten through it—I was just there. My doctor kept me sedated most of the time and so I guess if it hadn't been for Johnny Cash . . . he chartered a plane and came in."

She said Cash prevented people from stealing souvenirs from her home.

Billy Jean Horton entered a lawsuit in 1968 to claim what she alleged were her parts of royalties owed to her for Hank's songs. It was a ten-year court battle.

Her life basically shut down, she said, when her dad died in a head-on collision en route to see her. She had grown weary of burying loved ones. She rarely left her house, and became a semi-recluse surrounded

by maids and a chauffeur. All the fight in her was
gone. She thought.

On September 15, 1996, she discovered there
was still some fire left in her furnace.

Billy Jean Horton was jostled from a sound sleep
at 10:00 A.M. and saw three men towering above her
bed. Each wore a mask, each held a pistol to her head.

Her first impulse was to scream for her maid and
chauffeur, not knowing that the intruders had earlier
tied their arms and legs and bound their mouths with
duct tape.

In seconds, they did the same to Billy Jean, but
not before demanding that she give them the combination to her safe.

She truly thought she was going to die, and
recited the numbers. The robbers took $250,000 in
cash, along with a million dollars' worth of jewelry,
much of it, she recalled, given to her by Hank
Williams and Johnny Horton.

As the three men fiddled with the safe, the one
guarding her turned his glance. Ever so gradually, a
woman who was bound and gagged eased silently
toward the pistol adjacent to her bed. She had one
gun against their three. She thought she might die in
the shooting. She was willing to do so before surren-
dering her belongings, and her household, to common thieves.

One of the men noticed her movement and
stopped her before she got the gun that might have
resulted in death for one of the robbers and almost
certainly for her.

No one, she said, but no one, was going to rob her inside her own home.

Billy was a long time recovering from the loss, and more specifically, the trauma. She didn't leave her home for eight months. She surmises that she still sits up all night as a result of the intrusion. She isn't as comfortable as she once was when closing her eyes. Security and electronic surveillance were beefed up at her house.

"My place is now a compound," she said. "A gnat couldn't fly through this place without setting off an alarm."

And so life goes on for the widow of the most famous, controversial, and creative country singer/songwriter who ever lived. Billy Jean doesn't think a lot about her material loss from the armed robbery. There was never an arrest, nothing was recovered.

"I don't give a ratshit about those material things," she said. "At my age, I can put on a sweatshirt and blue jeans and go on. I don't care."

She said she is still wealthy, as she makes a "ton of money" off royalties from Hank's and Johnny's music. She invests well, she said, and spends the rest of her time raising her granddaughter. She said she has to give the fourteen-year-old her focus.

"I'm the only stable human being she's ever been around."

16

I met Wynonna through officials at MCA Records, George's and her record label. She and George later played on the same charity softball team. Arch Kelley, Wynonna's first and only husband, is a friend of one of my sons-in-law. Wynonna's children attend preschool with my grandchildren. She and her family have become frequent guests in my home, where we've had chats that resulted in the following profile.

The majority of this book has dealt with wives who've kept the home fires going while their celebrity husbands held the spotlight. I thought it would be interesting to look at a celebrity marriage in reverse. I wanted Wynonna in these pages because she is herself a star—a megastar. How does she balance stardom, motherhood, and being a Nashville wife?

Wynonna is thirty minutes late for an appointment that she has postponed three times. She arrives with no makeup for an interview that, for fifteen minutes, largely lacks a traditional element: questions. Tom

Carter simply turns on a tape recorder and she starts talking, rattling off bits and pieces of a story that would fill ten years' worth of daily drama without one rerun. Many wives, when asked, hesitate to discuss the information that Wynonna freely volunteers. She calls herself an "open person."

Later today, she'll meet her band for the first day's rehearsal for her 1998 tour, then have dinner with a fan who paid $2,500 to charity for the privilege. She'll finish the day with two hours of kickboxing. The entire schedule will be mixed with motherhood.

She has two speeds: rapid and blinding. People in the industry call her "Hurricane Wy."

Compared to Wynonna's force, El Niño seems like a soft summer shower. She is energy in overdrive.

Wynonna is perhaps the most misunderstood woman in country music. Onstage, she seems fiercely independent, almost sinister, as she growls her lyrics through snarls under rolling eyes. Offstage, she seems more like a gentle but free spirit—a child in a woman's body. Wynonna is proof positive that teddy bears have red hair.

This is a woman who played before 250,000 fans in 105-degree heat at a Texas speedway in July 1997 while wearing a suffocating leather top and Western hat. The outfit was definitely Beverly Hills. She was a Rodeo Drive Zorro minus the mask. She was stunning, and that pleased the fans. Wynonna loves to please, as long as pleasing involves no more than hard work without compromise of her artistic or personal integrity.

The same woman who sweated through triple-digit heat in leather was asked to come to my house to watch the 1998 Super Bowl. She asked if she and her family could dress comfortably.

Wynonna showed up in her pajamas. So did her husband, her two kids, and her movie star sister Ashley Judd.

Wynonna is unpretentious. One would never gather from talking to her that her first solo album, released in 1992, sold more than five million copies, and that she sold more records that year than any other woman in country music.

The woman who never mentions the statistics surrounding her astounding success calls me simply for girl talk—something as trite as the sharing of a recipe.

"She'll offer up her faults quicker than she'll cite her successes," says her own press kit.

She moved with her mother and sister back and forth from Kentucky to California numerous times while growing up. She and Ashley once went to live without their mother in Chicago. Being a child nomad helped prepare her for the traveling life she leads today, she said.

The three females returned to Naomi's and Wynonna's native Kentucky when Wynonna was twelve. They lived on welfare, with no telephone or television. Ashley and Naomi were dramatic, and Wynonna became the family clown. She said that she would not have picked up the guitar if the family had enjoyed modern conveniences. She's glad today that distractions were absent. She insists that modern youngsters rely on technology at the expense of creativity.

She fondly remembers sitting in her grandmother's bedroom at age twelve and singing and getting adoration. She was hooked. She figured out that all she had to do to get attention was to sing.

She wanted desperately to be loved, and she carried her guitar virtually everywhere, hoping people would ask to hear her sing and reward her with praise.

Eventually, Naomi began to sing with her on their back porch. A duo born in rural Kentucky would one day sit atop the entertainment world.

I love to hear Wynonna affectionately recall her childhood and past. It's easy to like Wynonna. It's easier to love her.

I asked her to continue.

In 1978, fourteen-year-old Wynonna was traveling with her mother across America in halfhearted pursuit of a musical career. She and Naomi eventually made their Nashville debut on the Ralph Emery morning show, a local program, where the host forgot their names.

He called them the "Soap Suds Sisters."

Naomi by then had become a registered nurse. She worked in a Nashville-area hospital, where she gave a tape to Brent Maher, a record producer. He listened and liked. A live audition was arranged for RCA Records executives on March 2, 1983. The mother-daughter duo was awarded a recording contract on the spot.

On March 20, 1984, they walked onstage for the

first time in their life with a band before ten thousand people as the opening act for the Statler Brothers.

In 1990, Wynonna was undergoing the most publicized change in her life—the breaking up of the Judds, the duo composed of her mother and herself. Until Brooks & Dunn, the Judds had sold more records than any other duo in country music history. Their farewell tour drew sold-out audiences everywhere and giant ratings for the final concert, carried live over pay-per-view television. They disbanded after Naomi was diagnosed with hepatitis C, an incurable liver disease. Naomi has since entered remission.

At the same time, Wynonna was leaving her manager of twelve years. Change was definitely the only thing constant in her world.

"They say that in your life you go through changes, but you shouldn't go through them all at once," she said.

She had no interest in, or room for, a romantic relationship at such a turbulent time.

"So, meeting Arch?" she said. "I had as much time for him as I had for a shower. When it came to men, that was on the back burner."

She was flying first-class on a four-hour journey from Los Angeles to Nashville, and the man who would eventually become her husband was in the same seating section—with another woman.

Arch Kelley got out of his seat, walked without invitation to Wynonna, and asked if she'd like to ride her Harley motorcycle with others, including him, for charity.

"He wasn't flirting," she insisted. "You have to understand. I have a lot of men write me, send me things, but they're chicken. They never have the nerve to come up and ask me out, you know? They're terrified of me, which I guess is the red hair and feistiness. But what they don't realize is that there's a vulnerable person behind all of that."

Impressed by Arch's confidence, and knowing the Harley thing was for charity, Wynonna gave him her telephone number.

"I gave him my phone line, which is the number I give, you know, to the guy who comes to paint the house or something," she said.

Arch's companion was sitting alone in her seat, awaiting Arch's return to his, and probably an explanation about the reception he received from Wynonna. Who knows? Wynonna doesn't remember the woman and she never knew her name.

"This is how my initial contact with Arch began," she continued. "You hear about love at first sight. This was *not* love at first sight. As a matter of fact, Arch was the complete opposite of what I had ever experienced [physically] before in a man. He was blond and blue-eyed. I had always picked the musician with dark, long hair, very passive and very gentle. Arch was in-charge, come in the door, aggressive as anybody I'd ever met."

She liked that. Although she wasn't looking for a man, if she had been, she wouldn't have searched for another timid soul.

The motorcycle ride never happened, and she

didn't see or hear from Arch for two months. In talking to Tom Carter and me, it dawned on her that the motorcycle ride might have been a fabricated excuse for Arch to talk to her that fateful day.

"I'll go home today and probably ask him if that was just a line," she said. "That could have been just a big fat lie now that I think about it."

Arch, who at the time was a yacht salesman, at last called and asked to attend Wynonna's Louisville concert. He also asked to bring a friend.

"Of course," she said, "he showed up without a friend. How convenient."

She said that Arch parked his car in an unauthorized area beside her buses. Her crew members wondered who he was, or more dramatically, who he *thought* he was. They asked Wynonna if she knew the guy, and she briefly thought about whether she should have him removed.

She instead said he was a buddy, and later saw him from the stage as he sat in the empty auditorium during her afternoon sound check. She made no attempt to connect with him, as she had a date. She and Arch never visited that night, and it was another two months before she and Arch spoke.

She called him.

Wynonna was in Pennsylvania and had just ridden what was billed as the world's fastest roller coaster. She called the guy she'd met on an airplane and seen at a sound check to tell him about it.

"It was sort of this safe phone conversation versus sit-across-from-the-table thing," she recalled.

"There was a lot of time between when I first met Arch and when I actually ended up going to lunch with him, which came after our conversations on the phone. It wasn't like I was calling him to go—trying to do that thing women do when they charm their way, that wasn't it. I think what it was—I don't have a lot of friends who are off of my payroll. There was a part of me that appreciated being able to call somebody that didn't tell me what to do. It was nice to be able to talk to a man who didn't ask to borrow my bus or ask to come backstage."

She at last saw Arch socially, kind of, when he attended the 1993 Country Music Association Awards more than six months after approaching her on the airplane. She wouldn't let him come backstage, she wouldn't let him come onto her bus. But she agreed to go to an after-party with him.

"I let him do that but I was pretty particular about, 'No, you're not coming on the bus and there are no corsages here, you know, this isn't what you think,'" she remembered. "And I think at that point Arch started getting more aggressive."

They *finally* got together for a meal—at high noon at a restaurant on West End Avenue, one of Nashville's busiest arterial streets. It wasn't candlelight and roses. It was paper napkins and flatware in a booth with wooden benches.

"I didn't think he was anything particularly swell," she continued. "And so I left him that day and a couple of days later he asked me to ride Harleys."

She accepted. Why shouldn't she? she thought.

Her Harley was a "Fat Boy" (the biggest made), and Arch's was a Sportster. Hers was larger and faster.

They roared around Nashville, wove in and out of traffic, stopped in Percy Warner Park, and kissed on the lips. She didn't say if they removed their helmets.

"I went home that night and thought, Okay, I've kissed him, what does that mean? And, of course, I'm trying to think of a way to get out of this. It just wasn't working for me, and Arch became even more aggressive. I'm out on tour in Los Angeles and he flies out to meet me. I was intrigued with the fact that Arch was just so sure of himself. I appreciate aggressive people. There is a part of me that says, 'Good for you, way to go.'"

She said she was somewhat reassured because she had her bus with her. If she didn't enjoy Arch, she'd simply get on the coach for still another show in still another town. He'd be left with her memory and exhaust.

And she did get on the bus. And he got on with her. And he got off a month later.

In the meantime, her mother joined the tour just to see Wynonna. She and Naomi had long since stopped performing together. Arch was right there, smiling and comfortable at sixty-five miles per hour. It was rolling romance in bloom.

"'Who is this guy?'" Wynonna said Naomi asked. Naomi didn't like him, Wynonna said, and surmised that he was "too fast." Naomi was turned off by the very thing that drew Wynonna to Arch—his aggression.

"Nobody is going to get with my mom because I belong to her, you know?" Wynonna said, pointing out that Naomi is fond of Arch today. "I belonged to her, you know? I didn't leave home until I was twenty-eight. She wouldn't have approved of him if he was the prince of a country. She was really having a hard time letting go of the Judds."

"Was Naomi nice to Arch during their initial days?"

"There was no hugging," Wynonna said, "no 'Come in and let me fix you some tea,' none of that. It was more like, 'What are your intentions? Can I get a urine sample? Can I talk to your parents? Do you have a job?'"

She illustrated her mother's continued protectiveness by pointing to the March 1998 issue of *Ladies' Home Journal*. The magazine published a brief discourse between Naomi, Wynonna, and Ashley in the presence of a reporter. The writer wrote the following:

NAOMI: I want y'all to know my daughters
    don't chew or cuss or drink or dance . . .
ASHLEY: Or have sex.
WYNONNA: And if we do, it's only in the missionary position. And we don't enjoy it.

Wynonna said that her mother did not ease her hold on her until her wedding day.

"She rode me all of the way, right down to, 'I don't know if I can come to the wedding.'"

She thinks part of Naomi's reluctance to accept

Arch had to do with the fact that Wynonna and Arch had a child before they were married, and that Wynonna was pregnant with a second at the time of the ceremony.

"I had to deal with the pressure of being an unmarried woman in the South," Wynonna said, and pointed out that her mother helped her through all of that.

Abortion was never considered or even mentioned. Instead, Elijah was born to Arch, Wynonna, and Naomi, or at least it seemed that way to Wynonna. Naomi remained protective and possessive of her firstborn daughter, and her firstborn grandchild, Wynonna said.

And Arch just hung in there pushing and loving, not rebuking or running, from anything or anyone.

Earlier, the discrimination against an unmarried woman who was performing in her eighth month of pregnancy had intensified.

There was hate mail, handed to Wynonna by ushers from audience members right before she went onstage.

"My pregnancy just didn't fit in with the Cinderella story of the Judds," she surmised.

Wynonna drew closer to her church, where she had always been an active participant. The tabloid press drew closer to her, and often followed her to the sanctuary.

One or two pictures of Arch and Wynonna worshiping God inside His house were published. The couple literally had their eyes closed and their souls open as flashbulbs popped.

And Arch stayed right beside her.

He went on the road with Wynonna when she was pregnant with their first child.

"He went enough to make me crazy," she said, smiling.

She said she sensed that Arch felt helpless, standing in the wings and wanting to do something, *anything*, for his pregnant minstrel. But there was little he could do. After a show, or when they were at home between tours, he might draw her bathwater or rub her feet. She loved that.

"I'd cry before I'd go onstage and I'd pray and I'd say, 'God, you know my heart' and it brought Arch and me closer together. It's interesting, because I would have never given a man that much attention without being in that adverse situation. It forced us to bind together and to say, 'Heck with the world. We are going to have this child,' and it made us stronger."

Any remaining doubt about Arch was erased with his accelerated attentiveness during her first round of prenatal care.

"I was really impressed with Arch," she said. "He went with me [to doctors]. I think this is what really caused me to fall in love with him because Arch would go with me to the appointments and most of the men are sitting out in the waiting room doing the magazine thing. He would go with me and ask questions and he got books and he'd come home from the bookstore with books [about childbirth]."

The day Wynonna went to the hospital to deliver, she rode at speeds exceeding one hundred miles per hour, she said. Arch was driving. All the while, he was talking into a tape recorder and so was she. They made an audio documentary. She remembers that the tape contains her swearing in pain three times.

On January 21, 1996, Wynonna and Arch married. The ceremony was attended only by a few close friends and family, including Naomi, Larry Strickland (Naomi's husband), Ashley, Arch, Elijah, and their four-month-old, still in the womb.

Arch was again by her side during delivery, and this time, so was Ashley. The three rode an elevator to the maternity ward at Baptist Hospital. They were accompanied by a man in a cast on crutches. Ashley thought the ensemble was somehow wrong, Wynonna said. Through an envoy, Wynonna alerted her security personnel.

The guy wasn't crippled at all. He turned out to be a freelance photographer in disguise. Security men even saw him remove his fake cast and crutches. And he never got the first picture of Wynonna's baby, for which one tabloid had offered a $50,000 bounty.

Some of her protectors might have been tempted to hit the guy, but Wynonna wouldn't allow it.

She remains close to a Christian counselor, and was consistently advised against "throwing pearls to swine," a biblical analogy.

"I love that saying and that became my saying about tabloids," she said. "My Christian counselor told me, 'Don't play with pigs, you both get dirty and the pigs like it.'"

Wynonna's babies were born eighteen months

apart to the day. (Coincidentally, Wynonna was born in the same hospital in the same room with the same nurse as Naomi.)

Wynonna did not undergo the evil discrimination during her second unwed pregnancy that she did during her first.

"I think it's like this Clinton [Monica Lewinsky] thing," she said, referring to the president's sex scandal of 1997–1998. She said she thinks people just got tired of reading about her pregnancies.

Wynonna recalled that her mother had written in her autobiography, *Love Can Build a Bridge,* that she also had been pregnant while unmarried. She said her mother had definite opinions about Wynonna's unmarried walk in the family way, especially the second time.

" 'I don't know if you're going to get away with it twice,' " she quoted her mother as saying. "There was a lot of pressure from people. 'Are you going to get married?' I literally remember shutting myself in my room many times and going into prayer about it and deciding that this was a decision I had to make because I knew what my mother went through. She got married because of me, so, you know, I didn't want to replay that."

Regressing, she talked again about her pregnancy with Elijah, which preceded her wedding. Even while carrying the child, she had not surrendered to Arch and their love in the way that has made them the happy couple they are today, she said.

"What really turned it around for me?" she said.

"The day Elijah was born I wanted 'Judd' to be in his name, a heritage thing, obviously."

Arch did not agree.

The two sought the advice of their Christian counselor, who told them that the child was more than a name.

"He is a soul, and the counselor was right," Wynonna said. "So his middle name is Judd, and his last name is Kelley. It was our first victory, not even being married, and coming to a place of agreement. Compromise is a big word in our marriage. Communication, compromise, and compassion."

She explained that her compassion for Arch lay in the fact that he was the father of the boy, and his compassion for her lay in the fact that she'd gone through ten months of carrying the child.

"That was what really did it for me in terms of starting the ball rolling on the idea of marrying Arch," she said. "And seeing what a wonderful father he was at home made me fall in love with him deeper."

She smiled as she recalled how Arch, who had driven her to the hospital at breakneck speed to have her first baby, drove her home at thirty miles per hour.

"He is so protective of that child," she said. "I got to watch Arch be a daddy. And that was what did it. And I don't think I would have married a man just for the sake of 'Hey, we get along and stuff.' It was like Elijah brought us together because he forced us to look outside our own petty thoughts and concentrate on what's important. Ashley and myself have always been priority to Mom, and I saw that happening with Arch and myself [regarding Elijah] and I thought, Man, I'm ready to marry this guy."

The two signed a prenuptial agreement, and Arch's willingness to do so cemented Wynonna's conviction that she had picked the right man for her lifetime companion.

Yet, Wynonna confessed, the first year of marriage was tough. "Really tough," she said.

"Why?" she was asked. "Did he have trouble sharing his wife with the world?"

"That's not it," she said instantly. "Arch saw me kind of flip out about how to manage a career and be a good wife. I'm a natural mother. I'm a good wife and a pretty decent singer. But the wife thing—I had visions of baking stuff and that I should be home lighting candles."

"Did you have guilt feelings because you weren't able to do that?"

"Yes, a lot," she said, her voice trailing. "So I really had a hard time [the first year] finding my way as a wife. I had great relationships with my kids, that was a done deal. You know, if I went to the White House, they went to the White House. I don't care where I go, they're with me on the road."

But Arch isn't.

Wynonna said there isn't a lot for Arch to do while she is singing in one city and preparing to travel to another. The couple has decided it works best for them if Arch is a house husband, or rather a farm husband. He maintains their spread and forty animals while she and the children are gone.

"The road is not good for Arch's manliness," she said. "He sits around and there's really nothing he can do and therefore it makes him feel crazy. And he's not useful there.

"I'll sometimes get mad at him. I'll say, 'Are you going to come to this event?' And he'll say, 'I'd rather stay on the farm and get this done.' And I'm like, 'Okay.'"

Wynonna said again that change is the main constant in her life, then cited an example that was a barn burner. She told me that the man she had thought was her father for thirty years is not. She was told that by her sister only four years ago. Naomi called Wynonna to make arrangements for the life-changing announcement, but was crying too hard to talk, Wynonna said. So Ashley, on hand for moral support, broke the news.

It happened this way:

Wynonna sang at the 1994 Super Bowl and was riding from Texas to Nashville on her bus along with her manager. Michael, the man she had always called Dad, had called and asked to ride along. She found that curious. She also felt an unusual tension, as her manager, also on the bus, seemed to watch her continuously. She had no idea that the men were anticipating the announcement.

Perhaps Michael just wanted to spend a few more hours with the woman who had always thought of him as Dad before she found out otherwise.

Wynonna's bus had just pulled into her driveway from Dallas. Michael went into her house, and she instead called inside for her personal telephone messages. One was from her Christian counselor. The counselor wanted to meet with Wynonna at 11:00 A.M. That was fine with her.

She told Michael that she was going to run an errand, and now realizes that he knew all along where she was going. She entered the appointed place and, to her surprise, found Naomi, Ashley, and Larry Strickland waiting with the counselor.

"Mom just had that look on her face," Wynonna said. "I thought someone was sick. I thought Mom was dying or something."

Naomi sobbed and Ashley told Wynonna that Michael was not her father. He had not been the "all-American dad," Wynonna said, but for three decades he was there whenever she needed him. She had bonded her entire life with his parents, who she thought were her biological grandparents.

To hear that she'd been duped for three decades was mind-numbing—to put it mildly.

She soon thought about Michael's late mother, the woman she thought was her birth grandmother, who told her when she was eight that she was special. She suddenly remembered the drama of the woman's pledge, and realized she had said it knowing that one day Wynonna would know—would know that she wasn't her birth grandmother at all.

And then Wynonna was told the name of her biological father. As of this writing, in March 1998, she and her birth father have never met.

"My first step is to write him a letter," she said. "Because, I mean, I'm not going to do this on *Oprah*. I'm not going to make a big [public] thing about this. I'm going to go slowly. I'll do it when I'm ready. I've got enough going on right now."

She returned to the subject in seconds.

"What I love about him [her biological father] already is that he's never asked anything of me, never," she said. "I've read about him in the tabloids because they tricked him into doing an interview and he said some things that I remember. And I stayed in my hotel room and cried because he said he'd always been proud of me. So there's already a tie there."

"When are you going to see him?"

"I probably will sometime this year or next," she continued. "I'm working on doing some emotional work first. The idea is there, the want-to is there, it's just making sure that I don't damage anybody's feelings."

She said she had considered inviting her biological father to her wedding, but changed her mind because of the feelings it might bruise.

"I'll pick something else later on," she said, before her wedding. "There will be more celebrations."

I agreed. Wynonna's life, I believe, is a constant celebration.